WHAT PEOPLE ARE SAYING ABOUT
MATT SAYMAN AND *THE LEFTOVERS*...

I love a good comeback story, and this one has it all. *The Leftovers* is a great basketball book that shines a light on what true competitors can overcome with a solid work ethic and a drive that doesn't quit.

—*Tony Romo*
CBS Sports NFL analyst
Former Dallas Cowboys quarterback

Matt Sayman's book is an inspiring personal story of a student-athlete's struggles during one of the darkest moments in college basketball history, the Baylor basketball scandal, and its effect on him afterward. Ultimately, it is a moving story of personal redemption and an eyewitness account of the beginning of one of the sport's greatest success stories ever.

—*Fran Fraschilla*
ESPN college basketball analyst

This phenomenal story is heart-wrenching, compelling, and inspiring. I couldn't put it down. *The Leftovers* is a must-read for anyone who loves the game—and anyone who appreciates a gripping story.

—*Mano Watsa*
PGC Basketball president & owner

I watched and encouraged these players as they faced probably the toughest thing they had ever come across in their young lives. This beautifully written story is about the fight and determination they showed to help create the highest of standards for Baylor's men's basketball program. Its effect on Baylor Nation is still seen today.

—*Kim Mulkey*
Women's head basketball coach, Louisiana State University
National championship-winning coach at Baylor

The Leftovers is a must-read for all basketball players, coaches, and enthusiasts. Matt's passionate tale gives an authentic glimpse into the ups and downs of being a Division I basketball player and shows the true meaning of the word "underdog." I look forward to reading it again.

—*Alan Stein Jr.*
Pro basketball strength/conditioning coach, Stronger Team

Matt presents the amazing story of the extreme highs and lows surrounding a top-level collegiate basketball program. His insightful recollection of the struggles he faced during this journey were life-changing for him, and will undoubtedly become an inspiration not only for other young athletes, but anyone who believes in the power of faith.

—*Matt Garnett*
Owner, founder, and director, MGBasketball Instruction

In a most redemptive way, Matt Sayman reminds us of what it means to commit to something much bigger than self—a team. *The Leftovers* suggests that adversity is not failure, that perseverance is paramount, and that the pressure of sport reveals character, especially in the wake of tragedy.

—*Alan Williams*
Author and founder, Teammates Matter

THE LEFT OVERS

BAYLOR, BETRAYAL, AND BEYOND

MATT SAYMAN

WITH DAVID L. THOMAS

WHITAKER
HOUSE

All Scripture quotations are taken from the *Holy Bible, New International Version*®, niv®, © 1973, 1978, 1984, 2011 by Biblica, Inc.® Used by permission of Zondervan. All rights reserved worldwide. www.zondervan.com. The "NIV" and "New International Version" are trademarks registered in the United States Patent and Trademark Office by Biblica, Inc.®

THE LEFTOVERS
Baylor, Betrayal, and Beyond

www.instagram.com/matt_sayman
twitter.com/jamodipodcast

davidthomasauthor.com

ISBN: 978-1-64123-837-3
eBook ISBN: 978-1-64123-838-0

Printed in the United States of America
© 2022 by Matt Sayman

Whitaker House
1030 Hunt Valley Circle
New Kensington, PA 15068
www.whitakerhouse.com

Library of Congress Cataloging-in-Publication Data (Pending)

1 2 3 4 5 6 7 8 9 10 11 / 28 27 26 25 24 23 22 21

DEDICATION

The Leftovers is dedicated to the memory of Patrick Dennehy and his family. Your loss changed so many lives forever.

This book also was written with gratitude to our coaches for inspiring us not to quit.

I want to especially thank my teammates for going to battle with me every day. It was a wild ride!

To the Baylor Nation and Baylor University fans everywhere, thank you for standing by us.

And, finally, to my family and my teammates' families for enduring everything with us. You were and are our strength and support. Thank you.

CONTENTS

FOREWORD

Almost nineteen years ago, I accepted the head men's basketball coach position at Baylor University, when the program was at its lowest point. I prayed about my decision and believed God was leading me and my family to Waco for a purpose.

I knew Baylor was a great university with outstanding Christian leadership. My end goal was to build an elite basketball program that would be successful on and off the court with student-athletes who would represent our university in the best possible light. At the same time, I had no idea what the team would look like that first season because I was unsure which players were staying and which were leaving.

Matt Sayman was one of those special players who stayed. You didn't have to tell Matt, "Dive on a loose ball!" or "Sacrifice your body for the good of the team." He was always diving for the scoreboards, taking charges, and doing the dirty work necessary to inspire the crowd and help the team win. Matt cared more about our team than his statistics.

Matt was a senior when we arrived at Baylor, and our coaching staff was very blessed to have a person like him to help build and form the basketball culture we wanted for Baylor. I wish I could have coached him for more than one year because he is what college basketball is all about.

When our 2020–21 team won Baylor's first men's basketball national championship in school history, Matt and the other members of the team of "leftovers" were an integral part of that success. Because of the past issues that created the opportunity for me and our coaching staff to come to Baylor in 2003, our climb from the bottom to the top of college rankings has created a lot of interest in how we accomplished the turnaround.

Tragedy, incredible adversity, and fear had combined to create a perfect storm of what seemed to many like insurmountable odds for this program. But the story has, indeed, turned into one of victory.

Even as coach of a national championship team, I realize that stats do not tell the whole story. And the word *victory* is defined by more than the numbers on a scoreboard. Our society celebrates the champions—and Baylor Nation has certainly enjoyed celebrating our championship. But we would be wise to remember that when we all began playing sports, we knew the meaning of *winning* was giving everything you had and being the best team you can be. By that definition, our first team at Baylor consisted of winners.

The Leftovers is a key part of the transformation of Baylor basketball, and it feels only right that Matt should be telling this story. Matt's words provide an insider's look at what life was like for those of us who took on the challenge of picking up the pieces and moving onward and upward at Baylor.

The effort, energy, and compassion with which future players would represent the school and the family atmosphere our team was based upon began that season. The players who stayed at Baylor helped lay the foundation for turning Baylor basketball into one of the nation's elite basketball programs and a national champion.

Baylor players today know our Baylor program is based on a "never quit" attitude. That's the legacy the leftovers left, and I am honored to have been their coach.

But *The Leftovers* is about more than basketball. It's about life and what you do when life throws you something you don't think you can handle. I believe the guys from our first season know they can face anything. And they are all champions.

—*Scott Drew*
Head coach, Baylor University men's basketball
2021 NCAA Division I national champions

PROLOGUE

Oh, no."

"What?" my wife asked.

"The kiss of death."

Jana knew exactly what I meant. As a former basketball player, a current high school basketball coach, and a lifelong fan of the sport, I have noted how shockingly often a team jumps out to a lead like 9–0 or 10–0, or 11–2 or 12–2, and winds up losing the game. It doesn't matter whether it's a high school, college, or NBA game.

When my Baylor Bears sprinted out to a 9–0 lead over Gonzaga University two-and-a-half minutes into the 2021 NCAA men's basketball championship game, I immediately thought of the kiss of death.

I had been nervous before the game to start with. More nervous even than when I was the one wearing the Baylor green and gold, stepping to the free throw line, and either winning or losing games for my team. In those situations, I controlled the outcome. I lived for those moments because I had practiced for them all my life. But this night, all I could do was take my favorite spot on the living room couch and watch as my alma mater played for the first men's basketball national championship in school history.

I could have been inside Lucas Oil Stadium in Indianapolis for the game. Two nights earlier, my high school basketball coach, Tommy Thomas, had texted me, "Call me when you get a second." It was 10:30 p.m., so I decided to call him the next day. Except that day got busy, and I didn't call. We talk frequently, and nothing in his text seemed urgent.

Coach T texted me again Monday morning.

"Hey, I had tickets to tonight's game for you and was going to fly you out."

"I didn't know that's what you wanted!" I responded. To jokingly take the blame off myself, I added, "You said to call you when I got a chance. You didn't say it was urgent!"

Instead, I watched from home with Jana, our son Landon, and my younger sister, Becky. That was probably just as well. If I had been in Indianapolis when we took that 9–0 lead, all the euphoric Baylor fans standing and cheering around me would not have understood my concerned look.

They wouldn't want to hear about the kiss of death.

Halfway through the first half, Baylor's lead grew to nineteen points. As incredibly as the Bears were playing, I still could not relax. Gonzaga was undefeated, the number one-ranked team in the country. The Bulldogs rolled into the game as four- to five-point favorites—and deservedly so, I had to admit. They had a tremendous coach in Mark Few. They had everything a coach could want in a team, including the nation's top-scoring offense built around a legit big man inside packaged with a handful of sharpshooters from the outside. In the semifinals two nights earlier, UCLA had played an almost-flawless game against Gonzaga and still came up short.

The Bulldogs were riding the momentum of that victory into an opportunity to accomplish something no NCAA Division I men's basketball team had in forty-five years: win the national championship with a perfect record.

And sure enough, Gonzaga reeled off a great run late in the first half to cut its deficit to ten points heading into halftime.

I had a bad feeling throughout the break. I had predicted that Gonzaga run, and I expected another coming in the second half. I didn't know if my Bears had enough magic remaining to keep pushing Gonzaga away.

But Gonzaga could only briefly get to within single digits of us, at nine points with more than fourteen minutes to play. A Baylor surge quickly pushed the lead back to sixteen, and Gonzaga could not mount a serious charge the rest of the way.

With about five minutes to play, and Baylor up by seventeen, I allowed myself to finally think, *We're going to win this thing!*

My mind returned to my freshman year at Baylor, when we qualified for the postseason 2001 National Invitational Tournament—the consolation prize for teams with good seasons but not quite good enough for the NCAAs. That was our program's first NIT invitation since 1990, and we knew an NCAA Tournament berth was not far away. Then my mind skipped forward to the offseason before my senior year. Media covering the Big 12 Conference had picked us to finish fourth in the league. With the powerhouse Big 12 practically a shoo-in to send at least six teams into the NCAA Tournament, I could sense the excitement around campus in anticipation of us becoming the first Baylor team to qualify for the Big Dance since 1988.

Then everything imploded.

One of the biggest scandals in sports history occurred on our campus. In our program.

Punishment from the university and the NCAA was about as harsh as could be levied against a sports program short of the so-called "death penalty." My senior season would be the complete opposite of everything I had dreamed of: a new coaching staff, a turned-over roster, and no hope of being competitive. And just in case we harbored any hope of a miracle season, our punishment included a ban from postseason play.

I snapped back to the present and watched the final minutes tick off the clock, the outcome no longer in doubt.

With ten seconds to go and Baylor dribbling out the remaining time on an 86–70 victory, Baylor Coach Scott Drew walked to midcourt to embrace Coach Few, his close friend. The buzzer sounded, and the coaching staff and players finally could begin their celebration.

"Coach Drew and Baylor," CBS play-by-play announcer Jim Nantz declared, "complete college basketball's greatest rebound and rebuild with a championship!"

I watched in silence.

Through the years, Coach Drew had made sure that I and other members of his first Baylor team knew we were a part of the program's budding success. After milestone victories, he would text me: "You were part of this. You are part of the foundation from the beginning." When I attended Baylor games, Mark Wible, the team chaplain, would spot me and mouth one word: "Foundation." Fans would recognize me and thank me for staying to play my senior year to help establish the foundation when others had left for schools eligible to play in the postseason.

Three weeks earlier, after Baylor had won the Big 12 tournament championship for the first time in program history, a package arrived at my home from the Baylor basketball office in Waco. Inside was a T-shirt that read "BIG 12 CHAMPIONS" on the front and "FAMILY" on the back. Inside the letters of "FAMILY" were the names of every player who had played for Coach Drew at Baylor.

The six of us who remained at Baylor after the scandal were booed by our home crowd during the difficult season that followed. But on this night, with our fight song playing as CBS cut away briefly to a live shot of Baylor students celebrating at the on-campus football stadium, it all felt worthwhile. I had missed my chance to be in Indianapolis the night we won our first championship, but Coach Drew had made sure I and the others knew we were with him and the team in spirit.

Jana interrupted my flood of memories.

"Are you okay?" she asked.

"Yeah," I said. "It's just so much. It's come full circle."

I recalled the day eighteen years earlier when a young Coach Drew addressed his new team—the leftovers who had stayed—for the first time. He had bounced into the room with a spring in his step, actually excited to be at Baylor despite the media wondering who in the world would want to come coach us. Some of us players were asking the same question.

"You're the start of something special," he told us. "Future teams will have success because of what you are going to do."

I didn't believe the words when he said them. They were still difficult to believe as the national championship-winning team's celebration continued on my television screen.

But Coach Drew's words proved true. My senior season at Baylor had started something special. Very special.

And it wasn't only about basketball.

1

THE CALL

The June morning was much like the previous ones. Texas gets a head start on summer, but this was a beautiful time of year to be at Baylor University.

The alarm sounded next to my bed, and although I enjoyed spending a little extra time under the covers, my mother had instilled a healthy fear in me. In high school, on a random Saturday morning, I was in bed enjoying the covers' warmth when my mother flung open the door.

"There's this kid in Chicago! Already this morning, he's been up for two hours working on his game!" she yelled. "One day, you will meet him on the court! And when you do, he will beat you!"

"Close the door!" I shouted back at her. Mom knew the dream I was pursuing...and I knew her words were correct.

Now, here I was in the summer of 2003, living my dream, entering my senior year at Baylor, and living in a sweet, off-campus apartment. My full scholarship would have covered rent at a nice apartment complex, but the additional money my parents kicked in allowed me to live better than the typical college student.

The original building of the LL Sams Historic Lofts was a church furniture factory. The factory's eighteen- to twenty-foot-high walls and the fifteen-foot-tall windows had been preserved, along with the half-wood, half-concrete flooring. Announcements had once been nailed to random wood beams in the factory's corners, and the beams still had nails in them. I had placed mirrors along the long hallway to make the apartment look even larger. Add in a metal sheet-like counter complemented by sleek, black appliances, and my place had a super-cool vibe.

I stayed in Waco during the summers to take classes so I could carry a lighter course load during basketball season. I also worked out with our team's weight-training coach. Each season, a new group of recruits with players better than me joined our basketball team. I needed every advantage I could find, and working with our coach was one.

As an NCAA Division I athlete, I treated my body like a race car. My kitchen was stocked with healthy food and supplements to keep me running properly. During the season, I would compete with the best players in the nation's best conference—the Big 12—and I needed to fuel myself accordingly.

Old habits die hard, however, especially when it comes to childhood comfort foods. On that summer morning, I made my favorite breakfast of pancakes with peanut butter smeared all over and topped with a generous dollop of syrup. After devouring the pancakes, I headed outside with my backpack of books and dropped the top down on my silver Mustang convertible. My parents and I had struck a deal back in high school: if I received a scholarship to a Division I men's basketball program, they would give me a new car with the money they wouldn't have to apply to my college education. They bought the Mustang for me on my eighteenth birthday.

I was running late to class, as usual. I loved the *big school but small school feel* of Baylor with its 14,000 students, but parking places were difficult to come by. I often parked in a staff lot, self-justified by the belief that my teammates and I were like staff because we provided a service to our fellow students. I knew my thinking was wrong—and the parking tickets I accumulated swept away any doubt. But my tickets somehow seemed to disappear when I took them to Robinson Tower, where athletes went for help with academic and school business-related needs. I never asked what happened to my tickets. As long as I didn't have to pay them, I didn't care.

I attended two classes that day and then went straight to the Ferrell Center, our basketball arena, for an individual skill session and a weight-room workout. I loved working out. I considered my effort in these workouts as one of the few things I could control. They were one avenue to getting me closer to being the best player I could be. I dominated the workouts and left the Ferrell Center feeling good about the state of my game.

I stopped next at the Sterling University Parks Apartments, which was the place to be in the summer with its inviting, blue swimming pool right next to an excellent sand volleyball court. Basketball and volley-ball require good hand-eye coordination, timing, and lateral movement, and I treated sand volleyball as a phase of my training, especially when members of Baylor's women's volleyball team showed up to play. They had superior volleyball skills, but we male athletes could give them a run for their money because of our athleticism. Every day, I alternated between the sand volleyball court and the pool, working on both my skills and my tan while enjoying the university's female-to-male ratio that made Baylor more enticing for guys like me.

This was my utopia as a college basketball player.

I was a senior guard on a team loaded with experience and talent. In a preseason poll, the media had picked us to finish fourth in the 2003–04 Big 12 standings. The Big 12 had sent six of its teams into the NCAA Tournament each of the previous four seasons. The Big Dance. March Madness.

Every team started the season with the goal of qualifying for the sixty-four-team field. Baylor men's basketball had not gone dancing since 1988. Those of us who were currently seniors were in kindergarten then. If we met the media's expectations, our team would make Baylor's long-awaited return to the tournament. Based on the players we had coming back—including future NBA players John Lucas III and Lawrence Roberts—I considered the expectations legitimate. Our coaching staff believed we belonged in the tournament and would push us there. Then, hey, the beauty of March Madness was that once you were in, anything could happen on any given night.

I loved my university. I had loving and supportive parents. My faith in God enabled me to stand for something far more significant than myself. I loved playing basketball at Baylor, and I was very comfortable with my role on the team. Barring injury, I would break the record for most games played at Baylor in a career, although that was in the back of my mind behind the team goals. I was lean and mean physically, in the best shape of my life. Outside of winning the lottery, I couldn't see how life could get any better.

"IT'S BAD"

I had just walked into my apartment after playing sand volleyball and swimming and was preparing to refuel from my action-packed day when my cell phone rang.

"It's Blair," the voice on the other end said.

Blair Browning was my favorite professor, and I'd had the opportunity to get to know him well during my first three years. I was always happy to hear from him.

"Hey, what's up?" I asked.

"What's going on with your team?" He sounded troubled.

I sighed, wondering what those knuckleheads could be doing now. Professor Browning taught communications, and several of us basketball players took his classes. From time to time, he shared funny or annoying stories with me about some of the players he had taught.

"What are they doing now?" I asked.

"Matt," he said, "turn on the TV." His voice trailed off as he continued, "It's bad."

I reached for the remote and turned on the TV. A local news reporter was delivering breaking news:

"Repeating once more: Baylor Bears basketball player Patrick Dennehy is missing. All police are saying at this point is that foul play appears to be involved, and they are treating this as a possible homicide."

I froze in place as if I had been transported into a bad dream and was waiting for the alarm clock to rescue me. I don't recall what I did with the phone or even if I said anything else to Professor Browning. I only remember sitting on the couch and channel surfing for news on TV until I was filled with disbelief. Nausea.

College athletes aren't necessarily close friends with all of their teammates. Our team consisted of fifteen athletes from different parts of the country, with different backgrounds, tastes, and preferences. Wanting to avoid the activities some of the guys were taking part in away from basketball, I spent my spare time with a great group of friends who weren't athletes. For college athletes—especially at the D-I level—life can easily revolve around your sport, and my friends didn't want to be around me because of basketball. Hanging out with them provided me a bit of needed escape.

Still, what an athlete experiences alongside teammates goes beyond friendship. I compare it, but on a much less important scale, to what fire-fighters or possibly soldiers go through. A bond develops from enduring through something that alone you could never accomplish. Regardless of how many other differences you might have, you have in common the pain, sweat, blood, and tears of a college athlete's life. And that connects teammates in a unique way.

But on this day, my utopia began transforming into chaos.

Patrick Dennehy had transferred to Baylor before my junior season and, because of NCAA transfer rules, was ineligible to play in games that season. Although I banged up against him regularly during prac-tice, we didn't have much contact with each other outside of basketball. But we were teammates, and we shared that special bond.

A few days after the phone call from Professor Browning, Patrick's SUV was found in Virginia. He was from California and going to school in Texas, so *why Virginia?*

A few weeks later, another teammate—Carlton Dodson—was arrested and charged with Patrick's murder. A few days after that, in late July, the Waco Police Department found a badly decomposed body. It was Patrick. He was twenty-one.

Baylor basketball was in the national headlines every one of those weeks.

I could not begin to understand what Patrick's family was going through. I also thought of Carlton's family. He was in prison, and his one act had created a tremendous amount of suffering for many people. Unimaginable. Confusing.

It was bad enough that one teammate had murdered another, but the headlines expanded to include a scandal discovered within our program. Major NCAA rules were being violated. Media also reported drug use among players. Even as one of the players—and one who had been there three years, at that—I didn't know everything that was taking place within our program.

Coach Dave Bliss, the man who had recruited and mentored me, resigned. Our program would be punished for his transgressions—and punished heavily. I heard calls for dismantling the program for at least a year to get things right. Many of our top players, including the two who would eventually play in the NBA, left for other schools.

In just a matter of weeks, our coach was gone, our stud players were gone, and our talent-laden team had been dismantled.

Gone with them was my hope of ending my college career by advancing deep into the NCAA Tournament, much less even *playing* in it. Everything I had worked so hard for, everything my parents had sacrificed so much for, was gone.

The senior year of my dreams had become a nightmare.

2

A GOAL WITHOUT A PLAN IS A WISH

In fourth grade, I dedicated myself to becoming the best basketball player I could become.

Nothing I had learned about the college and professional basketball players I studied indicated their paths to success would apply to me. No one on either side of my family had played college sports, and I didn't have any seven-foot uncles out there who gave me a chance of surpassing about a six-foot-two, average-sized build. My parents and I discovered I would have to take a different approach to realize my potential.

When I had played the year before in the Berwick, Pennsylvania, youth leagues, other kids' parents remarked that I spent more time on the floor than on my feet. Hustle cannot be taught, and my parents found a coach who could teach me skills to go along with that hustle.

John Szella ran Pro Shot Basketball Camp in the middle of nowhere on the side of the Pocono Mountains. Coach John possessed a passion for teaching the game with an "A" then "B" then "C" approach that made learning easy. I hungered to learn and master the new drills he taught me, and he insisted I take my time and learn to perform skills the correct way. He assigned homework to me, and when I returned the following week, he expected me to have mastered that assignment so we could move on to the next. I practiced the skills for at least an hour every day.

One night, my family and I watched *The Pistol: The Birth of a Legend*,[1] the biographical film about basketball Hall of Famer "Pistol" Pete Maravich. A young Pete performed crazy drills and dreamed of playing big-time basketball. As an eighth-grader, he made high school varsity. I related as Pete experienced the pain of being different than his peers because of his basketball dreams. In one scene in a mostly dark gymnasium, Pete's father looked him in the eyes and said, "Your mother and I—we can't afford to send you to college. But if you dedicate yourself and use your God-given ability, one day you will start on the varsity team. I know that, son. And if you are good enough, you can get a college scholarship." Watching Pete well up with tears, I found the first person I could identify with who shared my dream of playing college basketball.

But a goal without a plan is just a wish.

Through Pistol Pete's story, I realized that even though I worked harder than most of my friends, I needed to increase my work ethic. My parents bought me *Pistol Pete's Homework Basketball* videos, which took individual skill training to a whole new level. I became obsessed with the drills. During the winter, I would watch Pistol Pete perform a drill on VHS, press pause, and then go into the garage and work on the drill until I felt I had improved enough to move on to the next. Between Coach John and Pistol Pete's videos, my skills were progressing. My improvements in ball handling gave me confidence and poise. Mastering

---

1. *The Pistol: The Birth of a Legend*, directed by Frank C. Schröder (1991; Campbell-Stone Media).

different types of shots and becoming consistent with my shooting separated me from the majority of kids in our league.

As I grew older, I became a basketball camp junkie: Duke, the local Pennsylvania colleges, Future Stars in Iowa, and Five Star, to name a few. I loved getting outside of Berwick and discovering what players in the rest of the country were doing. I specifically wanted to evaluate whether they were working harder than me.

At one camp, NBA star Jerry Stackhouse talked about what it takes to make it in the pros, describing his journey and sacrifices. I appreciated his insight, but I couldn't get past his six-six frame and God-given athletic ability. I sat there barely five feet tall and slow-footed. At another camp when I was eleven, I took on the six-eleven Cherokee Parks one-on-one. He towered over my slight frame. I gave him everything I had, but I was never going to have his size. I needed the blueprint of a typical, everyday guy who had forged himself into a high-level player.

I found one at the Word of Life Basketball Camp in New York State. The Price family led the camp with Christian themes surrounding basketball skills work. Mark Price was an all-star guard for the Cleveland Cavaliers. His younger brother Brent was a gritty guard who had to battle to stay in the league. I assumed I would more resemble a player like Brent after I hit my growth spurt, and I listened intently as he described how he had to do all the little things better than anyone else just to get noticed by coaches. He said he spent more time in the gym than everyone else, making sure he was first to arrive and last to leave. As he talked of doing whatever he had to survive in the NBA, even if it meant getting by on heart alone, I knew I had found a player I could relate to.

When I turned twelve, I became concerned about my future height. My father was six-four and my mother was five-eight, but I stretched to reach five-three. My size-thirteen feet made me look like a clown on the court.

One day, Coach John, perhaps to take my mind off my height concerns, said he wanted to discuss goals. He explained the importance of setting realistic and achievable goals, and then he told me to return next time with a list of goals.

He rejected my first attempt as too vague. I thought through different possible goals the rest of the session, and then with his guidance, wrote out three goals:

1. Make my school's freshman "A" team.

2. Make the varsity team as a sophomore.

3. Earn a Division I scholarship.

Coach John looked over the list, smiled, and pronounced my goals realistic.

Playing college basketball had been too big of a goal to start with. That was the end goal, but I needed smaller goals to achieve it. The new list gave me a set of objectives I could wake up to every morning and work toward, dream about, and achieve. Previously, I had hope; now I had a plan.

The goals proved to be beneficial while living in a small town, where it was easy to get distracted from school and athletics and into trouble. My goals prevented me from getting into mischief. They also gave my parents ammunition to motivate me when I didn't feel like working. With goals I had made to achieve, I could not let myself down.

An example of my dedication to my goals comes from the seventh-grade dance. I had picked out a dazzling wardrobe consisting of a half-purple, half-green silk shirt and a pair of black pressed jeans—without a belt, of course. Checking out my vibrant colors in the mirror, I looked money!

On the way to the dance, I walked past the gym. I could see the lights were on, and I walked cautiously to the door and jiggled the handle. The door popped open. I spotted a worn basketball next to a folded-up bleacher. For the next several hours, still dressed for the dance—and thankful I had worn black sneakers—I worked on my game.

When I returned home, my mother asked, "How was the dance?"

"I don't know," I replied. "I was in the gym the entire time."

EVERYTHING FOR BASKETBALL

Coach Steve Yoder, who ran a select team at the Berwick YMCA, provided my first experience with real coaching within a team aspect. He chose me to play on his team, which traveled to various places in northeastern Pennsylvania. Coach Steve quickly noticed that basketball was not just a seasonal sport for me and invested time in me. He was a master motivator, and playing for him proved to be a turning point in progressing toward my goals. He emphasized defense, the side of the game I knew little about.

Coach Steve had few equals in mental toughness, and he would do almost anything to win. After school, he would take me to the outdoor courts behind the high school. There, he taught me how to play Kill 31, a takeoff of the traditional game of 21. Coach Steve added one crucial wrinkle to the rules: I could not call a foul, ask for one, plead, whine, or make any indication that I was unhappy with any sort of contact. Coach Steve slapped my elbow during my shots. He jabbed me in the stomach. He tried anything to disrupt me and get me off my game.

Townsfolk must have looked on strangely at seeing an adult beating on a small middle school kid on the court, but Coach Steve's game toughened me up. I actually began to crave contact. I learned to play through getting hit without expecting a foul to be called. Eventually, I started forcefully driving the lane, looking for someone to hit. The physical training helped mask my physical limitations.

The bookends of Coach John on offense and Coach Steve on defense provided me with the foundation I needed. My parents were squarely in the middle between those two.

My father earned chemistry and computer science degrees from the University of Pittsburgh and worked as a self-employed computer consultant. Although we had occasional financial problems, Dad always found the money to pay for any camp I wanted to attend. He also paid for additional coaching, as well as the huge clown shoes I routinely wore out. We did not have much in common when it came to playing sports because Dad had been in Pitt's marching band, but I knew he would always be there for me. And he was, taking time to drive me to camp after camp.

My mother was outgoing and a motivator. In my developing years, she gave me a book she forced me to read: *The New Toughness Training for Sports* by James E. Loehr. I had no idea who the author was, but after a short time, I knew his book backward and forward. Loehr wrote about the direct connection between the mind and an athlete's performance. My emotions were evident when I played—often to the detriment of myself and my team. I was the point guard, and I could not afford for my teammates to see my frustration.

My mother also influenced how I went about my workouts and drills. Each day, I performed a three-part workout consisting of dribbling, ball handling, and shooting. I obsessed with learning new dribbling drills with one ball or two. The ball-handling training also included multiple passing drills; knowing I needed to improve the speed and power of my passes, I spent hours drilling passes against the brick wall of my old elementary school. The shooting workout was a combination of Coach John's workouts. I called my daily workout JAMODI, an acronym for Just A Matter Of Doing It.

I made the eighth-grade Berwick Bulldogs "A" team. My coaches loved me because I was a pleaser who was interested in figuring out what they wanted and why. I intently listened in on their conversations to understand the coaching side. I also learned how to deal with referees. Yelling or complaining to them rarely—make that *never*—works. What grownup enjoys having a teenager argue with and demean him in front of other adults? But if I was respectful and helpful toward the refs throughout the game, as my parents taught me, I figured I would end up having the refs on my side. So, when the ball rolled off in the opposite direction, I ran to retrieve it for them. If they asked me a question, I answered with, "Yes, sir" or "No, sir."

I landed another valuable role that year. Coach Bob Calarco Sr., who coached the boys' varsity, asked me to keep stats at each game. From my seat behind the coaching staff, I listened to everything they said. On the bus, I sat as close to the coaches as possible to soak up more information. Coach Calarco started asking my thoughts on topics he and the other coaches discussed. He actually wanted to know what I was thinking! I learned to pay attention when the coaches talked because Coach Calarco always wanted me to have an answer ready for him. Through my interactions with the coaches, my basketball IQ grew.

My social life differed from that of most kids because it was designed to feed my basketball career. I did not drink or try drugs. My parents were active in church, both singing in the choir, and I spent every Sunday and most Wednesday nights involved in church in some way. I had accepted Christ at the age of five, and faith was an accepted part of our household. I never knew anything different. My parents kept me away from worldly things, and I understood the promises of God. I did not curse. I did not kiss a girl until I was a junior in high school.

My relationship with God and wanting to follow His Word, along with my focus on basketball, kept me on a straight path.

AN UNEXPECTED MOVE

When I was fourteen, Coach Steve called and informed me he had moved to Texas, where he was teaching at The Colony High School in the Dallas-Fort Worth Metroplex. He invited me down for a one-week summer camp run by The Colony varsity coach Tommy Thomas— "Coach T." My search for the next thing that could help me accomplish my goals had taken me all over the country, traveling with my parents sometimes but also going alone to places like New York, North Carolina, and Iowa. The Texas camp was my next thing.

The talent level made for a challenging camp. I was not very athletic, but my skill level allowed me to stand out. Throughout the week, I was ahead in all the skills competitions and one-on-one drills. My five-on-five team won the championship. "Coach T" had a unique personality, constantly cracking jokes in a manner that showed he cared about us. One day near the end of camp, he walked over to me and asked, "Matt, what do you want from basketball?"

I told him the three goals that drove me to spend every waking extra minute working on my game. He appeared to be analyzing my goals. Then he directly told me, "That can happen for you here."

After the plane touched down back in Pennsylvania, I did not take long before announcing to my parents, "I want to move to Texas!"

My dad had flexibility with his job. My mom had attended college in South Carolina and loved a warm climate.

"We can talk about moving there," they told me. "But before we do, we have to discuss it with Becky."

Mom and Dad explored the possibility with my younger sister.

"Let's go!" she said.

News spreads fast in a small town. My class had other good basketball players, and despite being in a football-first town, there was excitement about our team's potential.

I was riding my bike down the street while dribbling a basketball as I had watched Pistol Pete do. Coach Mike Scala, Berwick's newly appointed basketball coach, drove up next to me. I knew he would not want to lose any basketball-only players. Coach told me his plan to place me on the junior varsity team as a freshman—exceeding my first goal of making the freshman "A" team. But I had watched numerous talented players ahead of me fail to land higher than the non-scholarship Division III level. Basketball and developing basketball players were not emphasized in our town. I needed to go where I would be pushed, face great competition, and receive the most opportunities. I needed to go to Texas.

But first, my mother wanted to check out the situation in Texas for herself. Coach Thomas needed to sell her on the idea that the move would be good not only for my basketball future but also for our family. Coach gave Mom a tour of the school. The campus was enormous; with more than two thousand students, The Colony competed in Texas's highest classification for schools.

Mom was already nervous about moving when she learned the cost of renting in Texas was much higher. A monthly mortgage on a home actually would be less expensive than renting.

At one point, Mom and Coach T were walking through the lobby. Sensing Mom's apprehension, Coach pointed to a stuffed cougar—the school's mascot—inside a glass cabinet. "Steve was supposed to feed it," he said with a grin. "Just *look* what happened." Mom laughed. Coach had succeeded in putting her at ease.

By the end of the trip, Mom approved.

I moved to The Colony two days before my freshman year and started school without my family because they needed more time to sew up our plans. I lived temporarily with Coach Steve and his wife, Stephanie.

Living in Texas exceeded my expectations, although my first few weeks at the school required significant adjustments. For starters, my wardrobe was way off. Fashion wasn't that important in Berwick, and we players typically wore our basketball gear to school. My buddies and I had flattops. But at The Colony, a suburb of north Dallas, students were image-conscious. The brand name on their jeans' hip pocket defined who students were and their social standing within the school. And flattops were not in.

On the first day of classes, a student said to me, "What's up, dog?" I took a cautious whiff of myself, thinking he was calling me a dog because I smelled. I also kept hearing the term "y'all." I shook my head when I heard it because, to me, it was a made-up word. On the plus side, my classmates assumed I was smart because of my northeastern accent.

The lingo and the culture were foreign to me. The only thing I knew for sure was that when it came to basketball, nobody was going to out-work me.

I arrived at school an hour and a half early each morning and headed straight to the gym to work on my JAMODI, which now included almost a hundred drills gathered from four years of camps and videos. Following each morning session, I went to Coach Steve's classroom to talk with him. I soon became known as "the kid who hangs out with Mr. Yoder." After school each day, I stayed another hour or two to practice with other players.

Everything *was* bigger in Texas, including high school basketball players. These guys were serious athletes. The Colony High School had a huge stockpile of great athletes because three junior high schools fed into our school. In Berwick, we had one only middle school, located just across the parking lot.

Most of these guys seemed to know where they fit in on the team because most had played against each other for years. They understood the pecking order. Now, here I came in as a new point guard from Pennsylvania, and the other point guards had to figure out where I fit in with them. I determined early to show that I had no intention of start-ing at the bottom of the pile. I welcomed competition; it was the rawest reason we played, and it answered the central question: am I better than you?

The athleticism at my new school ensured I would have to play on the freshman team. I was five-four, skinny, and slow. But my skill level shined through. Most of the ball-handling and dribbling drills I had mastered were foreign to others in our program. I had practiced many of the fancy streetball moves they attempted over and over, so I succeeded whereas they failed most of the time. Although there was a lot of competition at tryouts, I accomplished my first goal by making the freshman "A" team.

We had a good team, and I quickly noticed that I needed to get bigger, stronger, and faster. We played Lewisville High School, a huge rival, five times that season. Lewisville was stacked full of athletic guards who frustrated me to no end. I had to count to make sure there weren't six of them on the floor. By the end of those games, I was exhausted, and in truth, totally shocked. They had exposed hurdles I needed to overcome.

After the season, Coach Thomas informed me that I would be playing at open gyms at schools in south Dallas all summer. His decision meant nothing to me until the first time my dad took me to one of the locations and, upon walking into the gym, I noticed we were the only two white people there. In Pennsylvania, it was usually the reverse.

The style of play in south Dallas was fast-paced, sloppy, and hyper-aggressive. The other players tried to physically intimidate me, but it was their language that most affected me. I wasn't accustomed to their level of trash talking. The fear they created in me was one that Coach T knew I needed to overcome to achieve my other goals.

I was sick to my stomach with apprehension before my next trip to south Dallas. I didn't want to go. We were driving forty-five miles for me to play there, so I was never going to become friends with these guys, let alone gain any respect. I looked, spoke, and played differently than they did.

I thought back to Pistol Pete and kept my eyes on my goals. I used the experience to toughen up. I learned that skill talked loudest. I learned how to overcome fear. I learned that my competitors weren't concerned with how nervous I was, so I shouldn't focus on it either. Playing at those open gyms that summer prepared me to successfully play in harsher environments.

3

ALL ACCORDING TO PLAN

I received my introduction to Amateur Athletic Union basketball through contacts in the south Dallas open gyms. Let's just say it was an eye-opening introduction.

The AAU dates to 1888, when it was created to develop amateur athletes and sports. In the 1980s, a couple of prominent shoe company executives began establishing sponsorships with AAU basketball teams in hopes of building loyalty with the players that, down the road, would result in those players signing lucrative contracts with those companies.

By the time I got into AAU basketball, the pros and cons were well known. AAU had the best competition, but it also had become a business for adults.

At open gyms, I learned of a few "coaches" who wanted to assemble travel teams. That wasn't always the most accurate term for them, and I'm not sure what qualified some to run programs. Some of these guys' connections seemed to be more important than what they knew about basketball. The bottom line was that there was money to be made in coaching an AAU team.

I landed on a team that planned to travel to tournaments in Los Angeles, Phoenix, and Orlando. It apparently consisted of players...and payers. That one missing letter made a big difference because not every player was paying the same amount, if some paid at all.

When my dad wrote out a check for me to play, I earned "all-star" status—guaranteed! No coach would derail their gravy train. He would tell every player on the team that he was the best he had ever seen.

Our team played in the Los Angeles tournament and moved on to Phoenix. Then we were called into a team meeting and instructed to call our parents and book flights home from Phoenix because all the money was gone. Not only could our team not travel to Orlando, but we couldn't afford to stay in Phoenix.

The best news out of that summer was that I grew six inches. I had been so focused on playing basketball and working on drills that I didn't notice how much I had grown until I reported to school for the start of my sophomore year. I was a glorious six feet tall! My friends told me I looked like a different kid. My neck was longer, my nose was bigger, and I had a super-skinny build.

I had grown as a basketball player too. I could handle the ball and shoot better. I still wasn't very fast, but I was good enough to achieve my second goal: make the varsity team as a sophomore.

Truthfully, I was fortunate to do so. The Colony had five or six times more boys than Berwick, but most of the talent on the basketball team had graduated. Coach T wanted to look at some young players, and I benefited with a lot of playing time.

I struggled to add strength to my body following my freshman year. I lifted weights, but I didn't put much energy into lifting even though

Coach T and Coach Steve pushed me to hit the weight room harder. I wasn't seeing results from my labor, so I didn't work as hard as I could.

After my sophomore season, Coach T bluntly told me, "If you don't come back stronger your junior year, I'm going to kick your a—!" He meant it too. He demanded more physicality from all his players, and he frequently employed the expression, "Feel big, play big." He believed that gaining confidence and strength in my body would unlock many more possibilities for me.

As a people pleaser, I had no choice but to adjust my routine. I worked on ball-handling skills in the morning and hit the weight room in the afternoon, often with Coach Steve working out alongside me. Having him in my life was a blessing because he spent so much time with me over the years, sometimes just rebounding shots for me.

As Coach Thomas had said, my confidence grew as my body began to fill out. My added strength gave me a more explosive frame that enhanced my skills. I could make more dynamic moves, shoot deeper and quicker, and absorb the contact that had bothered me through-out my freshman year. I also became a better defender. Lifting weights totally fit in with my JAMODI attitude because getting bigger was *Just A Matter Of Doing It*. Taking the weight room seriously raised me to a level where I could compete against elite talent.

Coach T noticed, saying at the start of my junior year that I had "found muscle" over the summer. I felt great pleasing him after the chance he had taken on me.

One day, JV Coach Charles Freet brought me in to meet with him. Coach Freet had been handed control of our offense, and he told me the best thing for our program was to run the offense through me. I eagerly nodded. Then he leaned closer.

"Matt," he said, "I want you having a chance to shoot or being involved in the shot on almost every possession."

I liked hearing his plan, but I anticipated possible problems. How would the older players react to learning that a younger player was the offense's focus? Also, because I had never been in that situation at this level, could I handle the responsibility?

"Yes, sir," I said, not wanting to show any indecisiveness.

"Now, I don't want there to be any jealousy on the team," he continued. "But sometimes it's a part of it."

Coach Freet paused to allow that statement to sink in. I nodded.

Then, he concluded, "So myself and Coach Thomas are going to be very hard on you. We will constantly be on top of you about anything. Players will see that there is no favoritism. You may be running because of things that you didn't even do wrong and occasionally be kicked out of practice."

As a sixteen-year-old, that seemed unfair. But my parents had taught me to trust my coaches, and my coaches were giving me a peek behind the curtain. I would prove to them I deserved their trust. Years later, while reminiscing with some of my former teammates, one of them told me, "Man, remember how much trouble you used to be in? Coaches were really mean to you." Another added, "We used to thank God that we were not Matt." I just grinned, not revealing our secret.

Doubts arose when I was constantly getting chewed out both in practice and during games. But winning our first eighteen games reminded me our coaches knew how to coach. From that season, I learned a lesson that stayed with me throughout my career: trust that your coach has a plan. His plan might not align with your plan or your parents' plan, but the coaches know more than you. Count on it.

The concept was familiar. My parents had taught me to trust in God's plan. Even when His plan and my plan were different, He still was in control.

At that point in my life, God's plan and my plan seemed to be in sync. I was not shy about being a Christian. But a problem was growing inside me, unnoticed even by my parents. I knew that Christ needed to be on the throne of my heart. In church, idols—not just the statue kind—were a regular topic. I didn't believe I had any ugly sins or bad habits controlling my thoughts and actions, so I zoned out during those sermons.

Matthew 6:21 says, *"For where your treasure is, there your heart will be also."* I was a Christian and that was my foundation. But I worshipped basketball.

THE SUMMER TO GET NOTICED

We lost a few key games that caused us to miss the playoffs my junior year. I was selected team MVP and first-team all-district after averaging fifteen points, 4.5 rebounds, and 7.2 assists per game while shooting 45 percent on three-pointers. I also was on pace to break the school record for career assists. Despite the honors, I felt like I let the team down with our failure to qualify for the postseason. We played games in which it seemed every player on the other team was keying on me. I determined to make my senior year more successful, and the only way to achieve that was to get to work!

The busy select basketball schedule caused my summertime obsession with attending every camp possible to fade. Weekends became consumed with tournaments in and outside of Dallas.

I made time, though, to take part in a camp called Point Guard College. I participated in PGC camps three times while in high school. The camps were founded by Dick DeVenzio, whose name I recognized as a former Pennsylvania high school star despite being only five-nine. I knew drills and concepts well, but Coach DeVenzio was a basketball genius especially adept at teaching the mental side of the game at a deep level. He instructed us using footage of NBA and college players as examples of both the correct and wrong ways to play. I still consider Coach DeVenzio and his PGC camps to have been as impactful on me as working with or playing for Coach John, Coach Steve, and Coach Thomas.

I also made time for a camp that had me buzzing with anticipation. Coach T was good friends with Rick Majerus, head coach at the University of Utah. Coach Majerus's three-day camp was known as one for serious players only.

The schedule announced to us at orientation was simple.

"There is an optional practice at 6 a.m. each morning," we were told. "Each day, you will learn and work on different drills until 7 p.m. Then Coach Majerus will invite some players to scrimmage until 11 p.m."

Are you kidding me? I thought. *Six in the morning until 11 at night? Every day?*

They weren't kidding. And with my coach-pleasing personality, I was going to do everything I could to be one of the players invited to practice until 11 p.m. As for the 6 a.m. optional workouts, "optional" was not in my basketball vocabulary.

Coach Majerus invited me to participate in the exclusive scrimmages. For the late-night sessions, he rolled out an easy chair and reclined to the farthest position so he could watch with his feet propped up. Current Utah players as well as former ones like Andre Miller of the Cleveland Cavaliers came in to scrimmage with us—my first experience going up against D-I players in a game-like, five-on-five setting. I expected them to be more athletic and faster than players I was used to facing, and they definitely were. They certainly didn't take it easy on me because I was a high school player either. But I was surprised at the mental difference. The speed of the game was so much faster than what I was used to; there was no time to think, only to react. Yet, I had to react correctly each time.

I felt behind when running the floor with the more experienced players, like they already knew the answers to some pop quiz. I hadn't felt that small as a player since middle school. Each day of the camp was fun, often physically brutal, and always exhausting. I loved it! When I came home, I was so tired, I could barely do anything. But I brought home skyrocketed confidence because of Coach Majerus including me in the scrimmages. Plus, I hadn't hurt the games when I was on the court.

Most importantly, I had tasted how beautiful that level of basketball was. Being on the court with highly intelligent, skilled players all on the same page without a coach was like performing jazz.

Select basketball back then was more "select" than now. Most of the teams were truly select teams, with only two or three players from each high school playing. Coach T received a call from Mike Hatch, who coached one of our district opponents, McKinney High. Hatch also coached the Fort Worth Lions select team, and he offered me a tryout. I made the team, and I discovered at our first practice that his team consisted of star players from all across the Dallas-Fort Worth area. One such star was Logan Kosmalski, a big, strong, bruising guy who wasn't afraid of any sort of contact but had a soft touch away from the basket. Although there were great players on the team, most were even better guys to be around.

Coach Hatch was a tough coach and worked us hard. I felt strangely at home when he chewed me out, thanks to all my experiences with Coach T and Coach Freet. He also had a method for keeping egos in check and making sure we played as a team. As a result, the players enjoyed a lot of individual success playing within our team concept.

We played in the highest division of the Great American Shootout in the Metroplex, a tournament that drew more college scouts than most in Texas. A player could receive a ton of exposure by playing well in the Shootout. The coaches for the majority of select teams seemed to roll the ball out and instruct their players to go make plays, so it was rare for teams to have assigned roles and run plays. But we were different. Coach Hatch had us organized, and we won the championship, defeating teams with higher-ranked players in the process.

I was the sixth or seventh man on the team but received good play-ing time, and I tried to make the most of it. At a critical moment in one game late in the tournament, I was playing point guard and drove toward the basket. Logan was near the basket, and his defender slid off him to step in front of me. In one motion, I left my feet and threw a perfect pass behind my neck to Logan. Logan finished the play with a layup, and the fans let out a dramatic "Ooooohhh" at my pass. I hoped the college scouts were searching for my name on the roster.

Our team traveled quite a bit. In Las Vegas's big showcase tourna-ment, we defeated a team that included future NBA player DeShawn Stevenson, who played on a different level than we did. In the semifi-nals, we beat a team with future NBA player Gerald Wallace. Although we got eliminated in the Sweet 16, the experience was amazing. The talent level we played against was unbelievable, and countless college scouts had surrounded each court.

Recruiting letters from programs around the country started coming in to our players. Logan and I became good friends, and we kept each other updated on what schools were contacting us. Most of the letters were mailing list-type letters, written generically and tout-ing that school's basketball program. I could tell that I was a blip on their radar screens. But one particular letter from Duke University sent me sky-high. Although I had always been a loyal Dukie, I knew I was not in their league. For the record, I was never officially recruited by North Carolina, Duke, or Kansas, but it was cool to receive their mass mail-outs.

Texas Hoops magazine ranked me the number nine recruit for my class in Texas. Soon, I started receiving handwritten letters from college coaches, which were a recruit's equivalent of a Willy Wonka Golden Ticket. Handwritten letters meant the coaches had seen me play and were serious about recruiting me.

I tried to pay attention to which coaches were showing up repeat-edly at our Fort Worth Lions games. I spotted Doug Ash, an assistant coach at Baylor, at multiple games. He had been an assistant under the new Baylor basketball coach, Dave Bliss, for more than twenty years. Southern Methodist University showed interest, as did Santa Clara, Ball State, Akron, and Hawaii. They all invited me for official visits to their campuses. The schools paid for official visits, so they were offered only to top recruits. My final goal of earning a Division I scholarship was within sight. Coach T advised me to eliminate any doubts about which school I should choose by visiting my top five, the maximum official visits allowed by NCAA rules.

FINDING MY NEXT HOME

My first college visit was to SMU. My mother and I drove through the campus, located in the heart of Dallas, winding our way among the university's stately buildings and immaculate landscaping until we met up with an assistant coach. He escorted us around the campus, giving us a tour of the basketball facilities and other amenities. Throughout the visit, I wondered when I would meet the head coach. Finally, I was escorted into his office. We talked for a bit, and he handed me a binder embossed with the university seal, saying, "This is what we are all about." He also said he was looking at some other guys, one of whom I had played with the previous summer. With that, the meeting ended. As Mom and I walked to our car, we talked about how impersonal the visit felt. We were both less than impressed, and I wondered if all visits would feel like this.

One week later, my mom and I drove to Waco to visit Baylor. We pulled into the campus, and a man jumped out of his car and greeted us before we could even close our car doors. It was head coach Dave Bliss. He introduced himself and asked us to get into his car so he could drive us around himself. I remember thinking, *This is more like it!*

My mom took a seat in the back so I could have more legroom in the front. I looked back over my shoulder toward her and spotted a Bible sitting in the backseat. My faith was vital to me, and discovering that

Coach Bliss carried his Bible with him was an excellent sign. My mother had been thrilled with the leadership I experienced in Coach T and Coach Steve, and she had been praying that God would send me to a college where the coach would continue to guide me the right way. The talk of corruption in college basketball had her concerned, so she viewed the Bible in Coach Bliss's car as a direct answer to her prayers.

Coach Bliss gave us a tour of the campus, which was breathtakingly beautiful. Even though the buildings were impressive, Coach Bliss told us of a Vision 2012 plan for renovations. The improvements would start that fall, and upon their completion, Baylor's campus would rival any in the country. We met the university chaplain, Dr. Milton Cunningham, who seemed genuinely interested in meeting us. Dr. Cunningham was small in stature but not in influence. His smile was infectious. He discussed the university, its mission, and the significant role faith played at Baylor. I was impressed.

Coach Bliss continued to introduce us to other Baylor staff, all of whom were personable and friendly. Each remarked how happy they would be to see me attend their school. But the biggest surprise to my mother and me was how proud Coach Bliss was of Baylor. He was in his first year there, working on his first recruiting class, and already he was plugged into the university. We noticed he thoroughly enjoyed being a part of Baylor. He also seemed to be genuinely proud to introduce me to people, as if I were already his player who he wanted to show off. I'd had that same feeling from Coach T when he introduced me to his colleagues.

During our tour, Coach Bliss informed my mother of the life lessons he wanted to impress upon young men like me. He said he would teach me to play golf because so much business is conducted on golf courses, I needed that life skill to succeed. We met with academic advisors, toured the brand new Student Life Center, and then went to the basketball facility. The locker room and weight room were being renovated. I was thrilled that our team would have its own weight room instead of sharing one with the football team. Coach Bliss took us out onto the Ferrell Center floor and gave me a few moments to stand on the court and soak in the atmosphere. I envisioned myself playing in this building, on this court, with the seats filled with fans cheering us as we made our way through the Big 12 schedule and advanced to the NCAA Tournament.

In Coach Bliss's office, he made his final pitch.

He pulled out a videotape and showed me the offense his team would run. I recognized the Princeton-style offense with backdoor cuts and reads—a cerebral style of playing. Coach told me he had watched thousands of players and wanted me on his team as his point guard. He had inherited a senior point guard from the previous coaching staff, but he needed someone to groom for running the show in the future.

Coach Bliss paused, cleared his throat, leaned closer to me, and said, "You can do this, Matt. You can run this offense. I know you can." I knew I could too.

"Matt," he continued, with a look of confidence and dedication, "I'm offering you a full scholarship to come play here."

What an unbelievable salesman! If he had pulled out a contract and placed it in front of me, I would have signed it right then and there, regardless of what the contract said. He could have required me to give him half of my lifetime's income and my firstborn for him to raise, and I would have signed with a smile.

At dinner, I could hardly concentrate on what he was telling my mother because I was dreaming of playing in the Big 12, night after night. I had never imagined I could reach that level of play. In Berwick, our goals were smaller D-I programs, most likely Ivy League or smaller schools. The Big 12 was stacked deep with NBA talent and a lock each year to send about half its teams into the NCAA Tournament. Oh, and I would be playing against teams like Kansas, Texas, Texas A&M, and Oklahoma. The conference boasted seasoned, future Hall of Fame coaches. And there was me, Matt Sayman, starting point guard for Baylor, running the floor in front of all those fans...and players...and coaches. TV coverage. Games and highlights on ESPN. My mind spun with possibilities.

A sharp pain in my leg grabbed my attention. I looked up to see Mom glaring at me. Apparently, I was bending over and drinking through the straw instead of lifting my glass off the table. The kick was Mom's only way to stop me from embarrassing her.

Coach Bliss did not leave us for one second throughout the day until he hugged us both and we shut the doors on Mom's green van.

Mom and I had traveled all of about two miles back toward home— probably more like 1.2 miles—before I blurted out, "I'm going to Baylor!" Mom turned to me and said she had been praying hard that I would find a school that would enable me to remain true to my faith and values. She had been praying that a man like Coach Bliss would come along and continue to mold me and reinforce the same values she and Dad had. Tears flowed. So much time and effort through the years, and it was paying off for us.

We agreed Baylor was the place for me.

A HEART-BREAKING END

Back home, I called Logan Kosmalski. He had made an official visit to Baylor but still was undecided about where he would go. I told him I was going to be a Bear. I added that Coach Bliss told me Logan and I would be the foundation of his new program. Logan liked what he heard. What could be better than being on a beautiful campus and playing alongside my good friend on a team that would become a major contender with Coach Bliss in control?

I chose not to visit other schools; there was no doubt to eliminate. I signed my letter of intent with Baylor on the November national signing day, allowing me to play my senior season worry-free and clear of distractions. Logan also signed with Baylor.

My senior season opened with a buzz all over Dallas about our team. We were loaded with talent. Jason Hammock, who was six-five, had signed with Illinois State, a D-I program. He had made the varsity as a freshman, so he had three years of varsity experience. Brandon Thoman was being recruited by mostly smaller schools, including some in Division II. At six-four, he would be an undersized big man in college, but his height didn't hold him back in high school. He was incredibly strong, benching 350 pounds. Brandon and I had played three years together, first on the freshman team and then on the varsity. Sophomore Bracey Wright was one of the top-ranked players in the nation and among the best high school players I had ever seen. The game was effortless for him. Bracey, whose father had played for Coach Bliss at SMU, had been elevated to the varsity team midway through the previous season. None of us who played with him at The Colony—even when he was a sophomore—was surprised when he went on to receive a full ride to Indiana University and then play in the NBA. Then there was Deron Williams. He also was a sophomore, a thick kid who was a solid point guard. He was so good as a sophomore that the coaches moved me to shooting guard so Deron could play point. Deron went on to play at Illinois and in the NBA, and he also won an Olympic gold medal in 2008 with Team USA.

That was the core of our *high school* team!

How stacked was our team? After twenty-seven games, we boasted a 27–0 record and were ranked second in the state. We could do just about anything we wanted on the court, and I was having the most fun I had ever had (or would) playing basketball.

Late in the regular season, as we were preparing to make our playoff run, my back seized up in a painful muscle spasm before a game. The trainers gave me pickle juice to drink, but that didn't loosen my back. Then they tried to massage the spasm out. My back began to loosen, and

I started warming up for the game. Then the spasms hit me again, and for the first time in my life, I missed a game because of an injury. We suffered our first loss.

My back was fine for the postseason. Winning the district championship earned us a first-round bye, and we went into our second-round matchup with Mansfield High with only one thing our mind: the state tournament. Coach T had dangled that carrot in front of us the entire season. When we took the floor for warmups, we noticed the Mansfield players had all bleached their hair bright blond for the playoffs. I thought they looked like goofs, and their hair made us want to beat them even more. But the blond goofs upset us 62–58, ending our season way too early. To its credit, Mansfield played great on a night when we turned in our worst performance of the season.

I had a meltdown in the locker room, crying and pounding lockers. The coaches who had gone to scout the teams we anticipated playing in the third round returned from their trip. One asked by how much we had won.

"We lost," an assistant coach informed them.

The scouts were shocked.

I delayed taking off my number 11 jersey for the final time. I was the last player to leave the locker room. Four years earlier, my family had moved to Texas so I could play basketball at The Colony. I loved being a Cougar. I had a lot to look forward to at Baylor, and I knew I would love being a Bear. But we weren't supposed to lose this game. We were supposed to make it to the state tournament. And I wasn't ready for my high school career to end.

4

WORKING TO SURVIVE

I was long accustomed to looking for every advantage I could gain on the court, and my friendship with Logan Kosmalski gave me an edge outside of basketball when I headed to Waco the summer before my freshman year started.

We decided to share an off-campus apartment, using the money our full scholarships would have applied toward on-campus housing. Thanks to Logan, I started my transition to college with a friendship already in place.

Logan was the complete package. He was the number six recruit in Texas; at six-eight, he offered a combination of physical play around the basket with a shooting range beyond the three-point line. His father, Len, had played professionally in the NBA and in Italy. Logan's brother, Landry, had just concluded his college career at Davidson College and was on his way to playing professionally overseas. And, to complete the package, Logan was a member of the National Honor Society.

Logan and I met with an academic advisor, and I had no idea what classes I wanted to take. I followed Logan and told the advisor, "Give me whatever he has." When the time came to select a major, I asked senior teammates what major required the least amount of work. That's how I became a speech communications major. Not a proud moment for me, but truthfully, I was at Baylor to play basketball first and get a degree second.

On the court, I quickly learned I was not prepared for the transition from high school to college. I was an eighteen-year-old practicing against guys three or four years older than me. I felt light-years behind; for the first time, my skill level couldn't balance out what I lacked physically. I had accepted Coach T's challenge to work harder in the weight room my last two years of high school, but Baylor's weight coach was immediately frustrated that I did not know basic Olympic-style lifts.

"What the heck did you do in high school?" he asked.

I answered honestly: "Tried to look big."

"How can you bench more than you can squat?"

I looked down to break eye contact. "We didn't do that," I said sheepishly.

Because I was behind my new teammates, I had to do extra workouts—not mandatory, but strongly encouraged. My teammates were bigger, stronger, faster, and, for the most part, better players.

Welcome to D-I basketball.

During a preseason media session, a reporter asked Coach Bliss why he had recruited Logan and me. Coach answered, "They both come from winning programs in high school and know what it is like to win. They are both winners, hate losing, and are both hard-nosed. And they are both coachable."

I liked hearing him say that because I believed I *was* coachable. I did come from a winning program. What Coach Bliss had told me during recruiting and said to the media added up. At least from my head coach's perspective, I seemed to be off to a good start. But I was so ready to start competing in official practices.

Coach Bliss gathered us before our first organized practice. His main message: "I am not your friend. I am your coach." We would be all business, and our business was winning. Although Coach Bliss's approach was different than Coach T's, I appreciated his honesty.

All freshmen athletes were required to attend study hall, and we discovered that it was also mandatory for numerous other players. But the coaching staff soon made study hall optional for Logan and me. I believed they trusted us to use our time wisely.

On the day we received our official Baylor gear, an assistant asked what jersey number I wanted. I decided to stick with the number 11 that had served me well at The Colony, but I was told that number belonged to a junior walk-on. My heart sank. That number had been good to me.

"What is the next available number?" I asked.

"Thirteen."

"I'll take it," I said.

"Why would you want an unlucky number?" the assistant asked.

"I'm going to make it lucky," I answered.

The assistant replied with a smirk that I interpreted to mean, "We'll see about that," and handed me my jersey.

I was making good friends besides Logan. One was Jessika Stratton, a really cute blonde from Colorado who was a freshman on the women's basketball team. She played a similar style to mine, and she was a devoted Christian and a really good girl. The more I got to know Jess, the more I liked her. Like me, she wasn't into cussing, drinking, drugs, or partying.

Some nights, Jess and I met in the gym and worked on drills to the intense sound of Linkin Park songs. She believed in her head coach, Kim Mulkey, the same way I believed in Coach Bliss. Jess expected Coach Mulkey would elevate the women's program to a level it had never reached. We both dreamed of basketball success at Baylor, and our optimism and hope fueled us to work harder.

Jess and I were active in the Fellowship of Christian Athletes (FCA), and she got me involved in the Student Athlete Advisory Committee that visited local schools and addressed issues teens were facing. Our committee used poll-taking to help students become more aware of specific issues. For example, when we asked, "How many students missed classes because of drinking?" the kids could see whether their perceptions were even close to the truth. That question raised my awareness! When I learned the percentage of teens engaged with alcohol, I was so thankful I had stayed away from drinking. Not getting involved with alcohol had simplified my life.

Just as my social life started blooming, we opened the 2000–01 season with two exhibition games. The first unofficial game of my D-I career was against Team Ezybonds, an Australian team touring the United States. After being inserted into the game, I made my first two-point bucket and followed by hitting a three-pointer. True to his word, Coach Bliss gave me a lot of playing time. I played the third-most minutes on the team. My college career was off to a great start.

The intensity and focus during practices were unlike anything I had experienced. I quickly figured out that if I didn't always give 100 percent effort, my role on the team would disappear fast. I constantly bought into whatever the coaches wanted, competing hard in every drill. I loved showing the coaches how hard I was willing to work and that nothing could break me. Even though I wasn't the fastest player, I would push myself further than others. And from my high school days, I knew the coaches were always watching. Pre-practice, film sessions, even walking into the Ferrell Center—as a player, I knew I was always being evaluated.

In our second preseason game, against the Houston Superstars, I played thirty minutes and made all four of my three-point attempts. When Coach Bliss subbed me out late in the game, he hugged me and said into my ear, "We are going to have a great four years."

I beamed with pride. Coach was correct. He had brought hope to this program and university, and I loved being a part of it.

EXTREMES ON DISPLAY

We started the regular season hot, taking a 9–0 record into the new year. Baylor's 1911 team had started 13–0, and we had a chance to surpass that mark. With each game, I was gaining confidence for this new level of basketball. Our senior point guard, DeMarcus Minor, logged many minutes, so I didn't always play the point. But I still felt like I was contributing. Logan's play mirrored mine, and our names regularly made it into the press releases and newspapers. Together, we were having a blast.

Coach Bliss often invited me to ride with him when he spoke at local FCA events. I would talk for about five minutes and then sit back to watch a master speaker go to work. He spoke for ten minutes, and every group we were with loved him. On the drive back, Coach Bliss and I talked basketball. I loved our one-on-one discussions and being included in events that were important to him.

Coach T and Coach Steve occasionally came down to Waco for a game. Having my former coaches watch me play was gratifying. Plus, after most games, Jess came to the floor and hugged me. Winning games, having quality close friends, former coaches coming to see me, and doing FCA events with my head coach—I was living my dream!

We entered the Big 12 portion of our schedule still unbeaten, at 11–0. Colorado was our first conference opponent, at home in the Ferrell Center, and I had my first opportunity to learn how different Big 12 play was. Although we were confident we would win, it would not be an easy victory. In the final minute, we had to make clutch free throws to secure it.

To say I was nervous during the game would be an understatement. I could make mistakes in high school and play through them. Here, the stakes were much higher. I knew that if I didn't immediately produce or made a mistake when I went in, my playing time that night would get cut. There were plenty of other guys—more experienced guys—ready to take my place. I didn't have a great showing against Colorado, and although I was excited that we won, I felt a familiar sting: I wished I had done more for my team.

From my years at The Colony, I knew of only one way to eliminate regret. After the game, I went to the weight room and grabbed a bench near the entrance. The coaches would walk by the weight room to get to their office, and I knew they would see me putting in the extra work. Headset on and crazy music thumping, I exhausted myself in the weight room and went to the gym, determined not to leave until I had worked my confidence back into place. I was sending a message to my coaches—and myself.

Next, we traveled to Lubbock to play Texas Tech with eyes on matching the 13–0 start of the 1911 team, fully aware that road wins in the Big 12 were hard to come by. Coach Bliss had us all pumped up to take it to Tech, and we jumped out to a 10–0 lead. By halftime, we were down by eight. Coach laid into us in the locker room, and we started the second half with purpose. But we still lost by ten.

Coach Bliss ripped into us hard in the locker room. I had become accustomed to him cussing up a storm, but not with this ferocity. His neck muscles sharply protruded. His face turned a brilliant shade of red. He was gritting his teeth, and his eyes glowed a hateful reddish-orange. I thought he was going to have a heart attack. He picked up a chair and threw it across the room. No one moved a muscle. I knew he had started coaching with Bobby Knight, but now I felt like I was watching Knight himself in action.

Just when I thought Coach Bliss's rant would carry on all night, he stopped, took a deep breath, and said softly, "Let's pray."

Everyone bowed their heads as he prayed. I cocked my head to where I could see him out of my right eye because I would not have believed a human could possibly go from one extreme to another like that. The memory of that outburst stayed with me as long as I played for Coach Bliss, and it inspired me to work hard so he would never come after me like that.

Baylor was into its spring semester, and I was well plugged in. I didn't party with the other basketball players and didn't even hang out with any of them, unless it was at our apartment. I chose to spend my limited free time with like-minded people. At times, I felt my decision built up animosity from several of my teammates. They didn't seem to understand why I wouldn't party with them, and some thought I believed I was too cool for them. That was not the case. I had been raised to stay away from the activities they were taking part in. A fear—some might call it an unhealthy fear—had been ingrained in me. So, I chose friends who would make my decisions easy.

For me, trouble came when we made cookies or fudge and someone dared me to eat a large quantity. Seriously. That was dangerous territory!

I continued to accompany Coach Bliss to speaking events. I wasn't comfortable giving my testimony because I felt like most people would grow bored or couldn't relate to my story.

"I grew up going to church and accepted Christ when I was five at a Cubbies meeting."

Wow, that's gripping, I would think sarcastically.

I did not have a dramatic, life-transformation story. No ongoing battle with addiction. No abusive or neglectful parents. I'd had nothing to overcome only after leaning on God.

Coach Bliss amazed me each time he spoke because public speaking came naturally to him. And we always talked basketball in the car.

After a road victory at Kansas State, we went on a four-game losing streak that gutted us. One of the losses was in overtime at Texas even though we led by two points with less than fifteen seconds left in regulation. I had no way of knowing then that would be the closest I would ever come to beating the Longhorns. Logan played twenty minutes, and I played eight. Neither of us scored.

Watching film of the game, I was stunned by the depth and size of Coach Rick Barnes's Longhorns. They sent wave after wave of fresh players at us. Once we burned through our top five guys, our bench could not match up. Clearly, the more talent a team possessed, the more punishment it could administer.

Because my poor play had landed me on the bench most of the game, I made a decision to be different. Many players give in to the temptation to be bitter and sulk over reduced playing time, but that attitude works against them. In the PGC camps, Dick DeVenzio had preached controlling what could be controlled. He encouraged us to find ways to enhance every environment we would find ourselves in. I recalled his words: "Make the environment better because you're part of it."

When a coach stands and looks down the bench for someone to sub in, he will call for a guy who is engaged in the game over one who looks like he would rather be somewhere else. I wanted the coaching staff to always hear my voice down the bench so I would be in the front of their minds when they wanted to make a change.

During the losing streak, Coach Bliss railed about our lack of effort in practice. The losses already had his kettle on full boil, but he continued working himself into a greater frenzy. When the other players started to look nervous, especially the seniors—who I assumed had seen everything by then—I started getting nervous. I wondered, *How bad is this going to get? Am I going to get demoted and lose all playing time? Or will he kick me off the team and take away my scholarship? Who knows?*

One day, he began hollering about how our lack of effort was deliberate defiance. Then he started questioning our integrity. He said we had no respect for him or the program. Then at a fever pitch, he yelled, "Everyone in the locker room! Now!"

There was no place to hide in the locker room. We were sitting in chairs in front of our lockers as I scanned the room to see whether the other guys were blowing this tirade off or looked as scared as I felt. I saw straight fear on their faces. Coach Bliss stormed around the room, letting us know exactly and descriptively how upset he was with us. Finally, he screamed, "Who wants to go in a room alone with me?!? Who wants to go?!?" No one volunteered. Thankfully, he picked out a senior to go first. As he got up to follow Coach, I wanted to remember my teammate's face in case I never saw him again.

The coaches' locker room was down the hall from ours. We could hear yelling and screaming but couldn't make out all the words. It was brutal. After what seemed like a lifetime, the senior returned red-faced and, literally, shaking.

One by one, players trudged down the hallway. Each looked near death after his one-on-one. The number of players who had been chewed out grew, and I knew my turn would soon come. Coach stormed into the locker room and pointed at Logan and then me and screamed, "You two!" He didn't need to tell us what to do next.

My heart raced. We didn't even have names anymore. We were, "You two!" But at least, I realized, Logan and I would face this enraged man together. What a wonderful blessing!

I walked behind Logan and was able to hide from view as Coach began yelling at us before we stepped through the door. I searched for an escape route as Logan entered, but Coach Bliss was holding the door open and waiting for me to get inside. I dared not look at his face, staring at the floor instead. I caught a glimpse of Logan doing the same.

Wham!

The door slammed shut so hard that a rush of air sifted papers on Coach's desk. He moved around in front of us. In a low voice, he said, "You guys just keep doing what you're doing. I am pleased with both of you." As if he sensed I needed confirmation that a miracle had occurred in front of me, Coach added that he was excited about our future.

My head hurt. The last half hour was too difficult to process without exploding my brain. Logan and I returned to the locker room, but we dared not smile. We wanted the guys to assume we had gotten blasted too, or else next time, we might *really* get it.

SIGNATURE VICTORY

We ended the losing streak and won two of our next three games. By mid-February, we were 15–6 overall but only 4–6 in conference. Sixth-ranked Kansas was coming to town, with all-world coach Roy Williams and future NBA stars Nick Collison and Kirk Hinrich. ESPN was coming, too, for its weekly Big Monday national broadcast.

We came out onto the floor for pregame warmups, and the Ferrell Center was packed. I looked around to locate the ESPN cameras around the arena. Bright lights were shining on the announcers as they did their pregame intro. It was a surreal moment. *This* was big-time basketball. I had come to Baylor to play against the top teams and the top talent, and I was getting my wish.

We started the game playing incredibly, taking a 10–0 lead. Eight minutes in, I looked up to the scoreboard, and we led 23–6. I continued cheering our guys on from the bench as we ran up a twenty-point lead with seven minutes to go in the first half. Then with about four minutes until halftime, Coach Bliss pointed for me to go in. I stood and removed my warmups. My mouth went dry. I tried to work up some spit and couldn't. My heart was pounding when the whistle blew to stop play and I stepped onto the court against Kansas!

We had the ball. I worked around a double-staggered screen along the baseline and arrived at an alarming conclusion: I was wide open behind the three-point line. Normally, I liked to get in a few trips up and down the floor before attempting a shot so I could get into a rhythm. But open shots were hard to come by in the Big 12, and I knew that I would be in trouble if I didn't take the shot. I let the ball fly faster than my standard shot and prayed it would at least hit the rim. I had to wait for the outcome through a blur that felt like it lasted forever. The ball swished through the net. The crowd went nuts. I had so much adrenaline rushing through me that all I could think to do was raise both fists as I ran back down the floor.

A few possessions later, I was in a similar position. Hinrich was quickly closing out to me, but since I had hit the last shot, I thought, *Why not?* I released the shot faster than usual again. The ball fell two feet short of the rim. At the next stoppage in play, I heard the buzzer and saw a sub running in to take my place.

We went into the locker room ahead by twenty-five points, and Coach Bliss urged us to keep pushing the accelerator. We didn't need to be told the game was not over. Kansas wasn't ranked sixth by accident.

We remained hot starting the second half. Our two seniors, DeMarcus and Terry Black, were lighting up the Ferrell Center. Kansas began heating up too. I checked the scoreboard, and our lead had dropped below twenty. That was fine; we still had a huge lead.

Logan played a lot of minutes and played hard, but I stayed on the bench watching as, led by Collison and Hinrich, the Jayhawks methodically reeled us in. Our lead dropped to fifteen. Then thirteen. Then nine.

Coach Bliss called timeout after timeout, attempting to halt KU's momentum.

Down to seven. My mouth was getting dry again. With just under six minutes to play, Hinrich let a long shot fly. Swish—a three. Our twenty-five-point lead was down to four. I could see fear overtaking my teammates' faces.

We pushed our lead to six. Coach called another timeout. In the huddle, he told us, "If I had told you before the game that you'd be up six points with four minutes to play, you would have been happy. Now go out there and finish it!"

We did.

At the 1:27 mark, our lead was up to ten. I heard my name called and knew why. I had learned at a young age that if you shoot free throws and handle the ball well, you will be on the floor at the end of games. I made three of four free throws down the stretch, and with the win secured, Coach Bliss brought our seniors off the floor to crazy applause. DeMarcus and Terry had poured in a combined thirty-five points. Then he brought off Wendell Greenleaf, a junior who had scored twenty points.

When the final buzzer sounded, I was standing at midcourt. We had just upset the sixth-ranked team on national television!

I wasn't the only one excited. I looked up to a sea of students rushing toward me. I had never been on a court being stormed by students for a postgame celebration. I briefly froze. Even though these were our fans, the experience was more scary than exhilarating. I looked for a path off the court.

Coach Bliss had just delivered his finest moment yet at Baylor, and I was bursting with pride to be a Baylor Bear. Bliss told reporters afterward, "We've had our ups and downs, but there's no doubt the opponent creates excitement in our fans and in our players. We fed off our two seniors. Terry and DeMarcus played exceptionally well. It makes for a great day for Baylor. This isn't going to change the face of mankind, but it does give this team some incentive for the rest of the season. We've had a lot of down moments this season, but this should give us a new-found energy."

Even today, our upset victory occasionally shows up on ESPN Classic.

SOMETHING TO BUILD ON

Coach Bliss hoped upsetting Kansas would propel us to finish the season strong. Our next three games were broadcast on television, including one more on ESPN. We lost all three games. Then we lost a fourth consecutive game to Oklahoma State before hammering Texas A&M in the final regular-season game.

Our finish dropped us to the eighth seed among the twelve teams in the conference tournament. Our only certain path into the NCAA Tournament would be earning the Big 12's automatic bid by winning the conference tournament in Kansas City, Missouri.

Because of the huge challenge we faced, it was only natural to look at the entire bracket. The top four seeds received first-round byes, and the other eight played first-round games on Thursday. We drew the ninth seed, Colorado. If we won that game, we would face top-seeded and well-rested Iowa State on Friday. I anticipated that if we won that game, we would have to beat Texas in the semifinals and either Kansas or Oklahoma in the championship game—a huge, huge challenge.

The coaching staff wanted us focused only on Colorado. "One game at a time," they preached repeatedly.

When we arrived in Kansas City, we received nice gifts: a leather jacket, a traveling bag, and a cool pin with the Big 12 logo. The NCAA has strict rules, but the gifts were legal. For a freshman, the conference tournament represented a magical event. So much school pride was exhibited as more than eighteen thousand fans poured into the arena, most wearing their favorite team's colors. Right before tipoff, I looked around and spotted fans from each school. Of course, there was plenty of Baylor green and gold on hand.

Just as against Kansas, we started the game aggressively and quickly built a fourteen-point lead. The lead was nine at halftime, and all the guys were loose in the locker room. We were going to close this deal. But Colorado came back in the second half and had a chance to take the lead late. They made one of two free throws with thirteen seconds to play, sending the game into overtime at 78–78.

That loose feeling we had at halftime had been replaced by the feeling that our season might be over. We'd had the game in our hands and let it slip away. We were fortunate to even be in overtime. Colorado owned all the momentum, and I knew that most of the time, the team that forces overtime winds up winning.

The lead went back and forth in the extra five minutes. Even though I had not produced much during regulation, I subbed in near the final minute. With twenty-three seconds remaining, Colorado took a shot for the lead. I searched for someone to box out and saw two opponents with no one between them and the basket. I was used to rebounding against bigger players, so I did my best to keep both away from the missed shot. The ball caromed in our direction. In desperation, I lunged toward the ball. I gathered the rebound and came down along the baseline. The Colorado players aggressively tried to strip the ball from me, and one shoved me out of bounds. The ref underneath the basket called a foul.

The scoreboard showed ten seconds to play. The score was 84–84. I cradled the ball in my left arm and pumped my right fist in the air as I marched down toward the far end to shoot the free throws.

Here I was, a freshman stepping to the free throw line. With a Big 12 tournament game on the line. I was confident. And if I hadn't been, I would have faked that I was!

Colorado fans were doing everything they could to distract me as the ref bounced the ball to me. I followed the same free throw routine I had established in fourth grade: three dribbles, set the ball at my right shoulder, bend my right wrist beneath the ball, deep breath, allow my eyes to adjust to the rim, up, and release. The ball kissed every part of the rim before dropping through the net. My second shot was all net, and our crowd erupted. After Colorado's desperate, off-balance three-pointer for the win missed, our fans, coaches, and players celebrated the victory.

The next afternoon, we played Iowa State, the number one seed. Most of the Iowa State fans had purchased tickets for the entire weekend, anticipating their seventh-ranked Cyclones, led by future NBA player Jamaal Tinsley, would advance through the bracket. We shocked their fans, winning 62–49. I remember their fans' frustrated looks at us in the team hotel later that evening. I didn't dare ask any what they were going to do with their tickets.

The following morning, the local newspaper described our win over Iowa State as the biggest upset in Big 12 Tournament history. Two steps into our huge challenge, we were confident that we could forge our way into the postseason. Now, we just needed to defeat Texas and the winner of the other semifinal between Kansas and Oklahoma.

But playing for a third consecutive day, we just didn't have the legs to stay with Texas. The Longhorns led us from start to finish. We managed to make a good run at them late, but they held us off and won 76–62.

Our postseason fate would be determined by the NCAA Tournament selection committee. We had entered the conference tournament believing we needed to win all four games to make the field of sixty-four teams. But we knew the win over Iowa State would get us some attention. Then we hoped the committee would look at our entire body of work, not just our conference record. After all, we had a nice-looking 19–11 record. I couldn't believe that in my first year of college basketball, I had a chance of playing in the Big Dance.

Back home in Waco, we waited anxiously for the news. The committee didn't select us. I felt for DeMarcus and Terry, our seniors, and vowed that I would have my chance on the big stage before my four years were up.

Then we received a gift. The NIT invited us into its tournament. Sadness turned to joy. There was no feeling like being selected to play in a postseason tournament. And the NIT had paired us with New Mexico, the team Coach Bliss coached for eleven years before taking the Baylor job. Talk about a storybook first-round matchup! He had led the Lobos to seven NCAA tournaments and was the program's all-time winningest coach, with 246 victories. His teams won at least twenty games in a season ten times. He was that good of a coach, and now he was starting to accomplish at Baylor what he had at New Mexico.

But we would have to travel to Albuquerque to play in one of college basketball's most hostile environments. During our preparations, I could tell Coach Bliss really wanted to win this game. When he walked out of The Pit's long tunnel leading to the visiting team's bench, half of the people in the arena cheered and the other half booed.

The Pit was bizarre because it was built into the ground, and we had to walk *down* to floor level when we entered. The atmosphere was unlike any I had experienced. The fans were so loud that I could not hear someone standing next to me screaming into my ear. Like all good teams, the Lobos—coached by Fran Fraschilla, the current ESPN college basketball analyst—fed off their fans' energy.

My first possession in the game, I got called for a ten-second violation against their full-court pressure. Their players were so fast that I couldn't even get the ball across half-court.

We lost by ten. We could not reward Coach Bliss for his decision to come to Baylor. I was disappointed we didn't give him the win that I could tell he so badly wanted.

My freshman season ended with great experiences in the bank. Plus, we all received cool watches for playing in the NIT.

As the summer approached, our group of returning players was excited. Coach Bliss was known for turning around programs at Oklahoma, SMU, and New Mexico before coming to Baylor. His hiring had brought hope to downtrodden Bears fans. Two seasons in, and he had already produced a postseason tournament appearance. Greater things were to come.

Who knew how far Coach Bliss could lead us? I trusted him, and I would follow him every step of the way.

5

RIDING THE
ROLLER COASTER

Coach Ash asking to meet with Logan and me seemed strange. As Coach Bliss's right-hand man, Coach Ash was more seen than heard. Logan and I reported to his office unsure of what to expect.

"Guys," he began, "just wanted to explain how the transition from season to season works. Although we are very happy with both of you, we have to continue to recruit year after year. Matt, we will need to get another point guard to play. We can't have just one."

I understood, although it was startling to hear a coach talk about recruiting for my position. Coach Ash was a veteran coach, so he probably knew my thoughts.

"I do not want you to worry about your position here," he told me. "Just keep working hard and know that no matter who we bring in, you will have a lot more experience than them."

As Logan and I left Coach Ash's office, the secretary stopped us.

"Matt, Coach Bliss wants to see you."

I must have shot Logan a worried look because he grinned like everything was okay and left.

Coach Bliss was poring over information on his desk when I walked in.

"What are you right now, 200?" Coach Bliss asked, referring to my weight.

"I'm 210," I responded.

"Matt, I want to move you to point guard next season. And to do that, I need you faster and quicker. I need you to get to 190."

DeMarcus had started every game at point guard the previous season and led the team in minutes played. Most of my minutes came at shooting guard. I swallowed hard. I had worked my tail off to put on weight so I could compete as a two or a three against the monsters of the Big 12.

"Can you do that?" Coach asked.

He wasn't asking for my opinion. I could either accept this mission or choose to go elsewhere. I hadn't weighed 190 since my junior year in high school. With a frame that had little fat, losing twenty pounds would mean losing muscle mass, and that would require a ton of work in the gym.

The people-pleaser in me responded, "Yes, sir. No problem."

Coach folded his hands on his desk and smiled his approval. He appeared confident.

"Matt, I want to thank you for everything that you do."

With that one comment, Coach Bliss eliminated any doubt I had about my future at Baylor. He wanted me there and appreciated what I contributed to his program.

During the recruiting process, I had assumed D-I scholarships were full rides for four years. But I had been talking to teammates and players on other Big 12 teams recently and also had taken note of players who quit or were suspended, terminated, or transferred. I learned that scholarships were year to year instead of guaranteed for four years. When a student-athlete received a full ride, he or she actually received a one-year full ride with three one-year options the school could renew. Scholarships had to be earned each year, or a student-athlete could be cut. That helped to explain why players around the conference had seemingly disappeared from their teams.

Each year, I would receive paperwork notifying me that Baylor had picked up another option year on my scholarship. After learning more about scholarships, the reality that I could be cut was constantly in the back of my mind. I was always being evaluated, and that served to drive me harder.

The reality of Coach Ash's comments became apparent a few days later when Baylor received a commitment from Lawrence Roberts, a six-nine, highly coveted forward from Houston. Roberts played Logan's position. I wondered whether Logan and I were being recruited over. If our coaches did that to Logan, they could easily do the same to me.

Sure enough, in a few more days, I learned that John Lucas III, also from Houston, announced he was coming to Baylor. Lucas played point guard.

As I read Lucas's bio, my anxiety mounted. He had scored 3,300 points in his high school career and averaged over thirty points per game one season. His dad had played fourteen seasons in the NBA. Lucas was almost the exact opposite of me. At five-eleven and 155 pounds, he was small, but he was lightning fast. I was not much of a scoring threat at point guard. Lucas was. I was the typical point guard who ran an offense in a way that created scoring opportunities for others. But when a team had a point guard that could score a bunch of points, opposing teams would have to focus on him. That would free up his teammates by taking away some of the defensive help on them.

I reminded myself that star high school players didn't always pan out. College was a different ballgame. Players could make their way into the coach's doghouse and not play, or they could struggle with their grades and lose eligibility. I could have probably listed a dozen ways players could make some kind of mistake and not play. I took a deep breath and remembered what the coaches had told me: work extra hard this summer and lose weight. Everything else was out of my control. Most importantly, if the two new players worked out, we were going to have an awesome team. I needed to make sure I was on the team and playing.

Basketball was business, and I approached it that way. I ate chicken breast sandwiches all summer. I wrote down everything I ate and monitored my protein intake. I cut out all junk food—no more all-you-can-eat fudge and cookie dares—and burned calories like my job depended on it. Because it did.

As weight fell off, I felt a step quicker. Veins started popping in my shoulders, which motivated me even more. I was in the best shape of my life.

By the end of the summer, I weighed 190. I showed up to fall workouts prepared. I wasn't sure how good John was or what type of teammate he would be, but he would get my best in competing for the starting point guard position.

From individual workouts and pickup ball at the Ferrell Center, I could tell John and Lawrence upgraded our team. Our previous season's success also enabled our coaches to recruit Kenny Taylor, an outstanding three-point shooter. Kenny's impressive resume included being part of back-to-back Texas high school state championships at Sugar Land Willowridge. There, he teamed with T.J. Ford, a phenomenal point guard who had signed to play at Texas.

John and I initially mixed about as well as oil and water. His individualistic personality clashed with my Baylor-first attitude. In a pickup game one fall day, I went up for a three-pointer as John closed out hard toward me. I released the shot and felt a sharp pain as John buried a fist into my leg as he ran past me. Even with the weight I had lost, I still had thirty-five pounds on him, and I shoved him as hard as I could. John didn't back down, though. Not everyone liked John, but no one denied he could play.

On the day practices began, Coach Bliss was the happiest I had seen him since he had signed a contract extension during the twelve-game winning streak my freshman season. Following introductions and welcomes, Coach's face transformed to his get-down-to-business expression. He started in with the same speech he had given to start the year before: he was not our friend; he was our coach. We had enough friends; he would teach us basketball. This was all business, and our business was winning.

I came to a harsh realization in the first few practices that all the weight I had lost would not make me better than John. He was too fast and too quick. He would be starting ahead of me. I had anticipated starting at point guard this season, and as a competitor, it was difficult to realize my hard work wasn't enough to take over the starting spot.

I spent the next few days questioning my future at Baylor. Thankfully, my time at PGC camps had given me the skills I needed to handle a situation like this. I had to identify what I could and could not control, find new ways to impact the team, and remain consistent. Being a team player had worked in the past. I would support my coaches and teammates. I would be a cheerleader during games while waiting for my opportunity, which I had noticed invariably seemed to come for those who were prepared. No matter how I felt about not starting, my effort would not falter; I would still aim to work harder than everyone else. Then when my name was called, I would be ready.

Outside of basketball, I had a great group of friends who were well-rounded and like-minded. I was unashamed of my Christianity, even though that sometimes meant feeling out of place in the locker room. My friends and I attended church together. With so many opportunities for college students to get into trouble, we had our own fun that didn't compromise our values.

I was pretty well known around campus for my beliefs. On the occasions when I did stop by a party, some people who knew me would hide their drinks. I wasn't sure why. Perhaps they didn't want me to judge them, although I wouldn't have. I did not have a problem with people whose choices were different than mine. Samson was one of my biblical heroes growing up. When he followed God's ways, he was blessed. It wasn't until he compromised that he failed. In some ways, my life had followed a similar pattern.

A few weeks later, Coach Bliss asked me to join him on a trip to speak to local kids. I never turned down such an opportunity.

On this trip, as he drove, he talked about Bobby Knight, under whom he had started his coaching career. He had a lot of good stories to share. One time, Coach Bliss showed up late for a meeting, and Coach Knight really laid into him. Coach Bliss chuckled as he said that Coach Knight was an only child and too used to getting his own way. I laughed just imagining Coach Bliss getting yelled at by anyone.

I loved hearing these inside stories from Coach Bliss. I wanted to get to know him better, but he was difficult to read. Everything seemed to be all business with him.

At the event, Coach talked to the students about the importance of prayer. He recommended that they set a schedule to pray and stick with it, adding he prayed every day whether he was at home or on the road. Coach Bliss made it clear how important he considered his relationship with God.

VALUABLE IN ANY ROLE

Even though I had expected John to be our starting point guard, I started in our first exhibition game, as did Logan at center ahead of Lawrence. In the second exhibition, John and Lawrence started in our places. For the regular-season opener, Logan and I were back in the starting lineup. John and Lawrence started the next game.

The pattern broke in our third game, with Logan and me out of the starting lineup. And for the next. And the next. John and Lawrence started eight consecutive games. Logan and I would get our minutes—I was playing fifteen to twenty minutes most games—but we were now bench players.

John was so talented that despite my personal feelings toward him, I marveled at his skill and athleticism. As I watched him night after night, I held out hope that I could win the starting job because he had a few weaknesses. Plus, many players with great talent get stuck with the dreaded "potential" label and don't work out for various reasons.

In a few games in this early stage of John's college career, it was apparent that he lacked leadership. A point guard is an extension of the head coach and must care about the others on his team. John did not have that trait yet. He also was constantly butting heads with Coach Bliss. John was not buying into Coach Bliss's philosophy and strategy. Coach constantly preached, "Baylor first, you second," holding up one hand to symbolize Baylor and keeping the second hand symbolizing "you" distant. I decided to remain patient, stay consistent, and bide my time.

For our last game in December, near the end of the nonconference schedule, we bused north to Fort Worth to play Texas Christian University. The past few games had been rough for John. He was still arguing with Coach Bliss over what he thought was right—on the practice floor, in front of the team. Big mistake.

We completed our pregame warmups and returned to the locker room for the final prep. Our routine was to go into the locker room, sit together, and wait for Coach to go over what he had already written on the whiteboard. I always felt prepared to play because Coach left nothing uncovered. He would write the jersey numbers of our starting five matched up against the opponent's starters. He also would have our offensive strategies, defensive strategies, keys to winning, and an inspirational quote. Sometimes, he diagrammed a few out-of-bounds plays the opposition liked to run.

When I walked into the visitors' locker room, I saw my number 13 matched up against TCU's point guard. John was officially in trouble, and I was in the starting lineup.

I was determined to show not only the coaches but also myself that I could start at point guard. I played out of my mind, making my mark all over the floor. Coach must have felt the need to keep me in the game because for what would be the only time in my career, I played the entire forty minutes.

On one play in particular, I showcased the best thing I could offer: effort. TCU's point guard had a lazy crossover. Anticipating his move, I got a piece of the ball as it went rolling. He unwisely tried to bend over and pick it up as I went flying to the floor for the ball. As we both grabbed for it, the ball came loose, allowing him to pick it up. From the floor, I reached and snatched it back, and at the same time, Coach Bliss called for a timeout. With our bench and fans going crazy for my effort, I stood and gave them a huge fist pump and yell.

Even though we lost 92–81 to drop to 9–3, I played the most complete game of my career to that point, finishing with fifteen points, six rebounds, and five assists. Although John hadn't started, he played thirty-two minutes and scored a team-high twenty-one points. He scored fifteen of those points before halftime. He had responded to Coach's challenge; he would not let being benched affect his productivity.

I started the next two games—including a defeat of Iowa State in the conference opener—but John logged more minutes and scored more points than me in both. Then I was back on the bench for the next game. Afterward, my parents were visibly upset and asked what I had done to put myself in that position.

"Nothing!" I said in frustration. "I have no idea. I haven't done anything different."

I also knew the truth, which anyone watching with an unbiased eye could plainly see: John was outplaying me.

In high school, I had played because I deserved to play. College was different. You play if the coach believes you give the team their best chance to win. Every night is a new audition. If the coach thinks another player should play instead of you, you're warming the bench.

I had to reflect back on something Coach T had taught me: "Don't try and understand why coaches do the things they do. Be a team player and follow their instructions. Just wait it out. Good things will eventually come your way."

I knew watching me not start was difficult for my parents, but I had to follow Coach T's advice to survive.

When I wasn't in a game, I was both a cheerleader and a navigator within the team. Wendell Greenleaf, one of our better players, was having problems, and he became a headache on and off the court. He was constantly getting into it with our coaches and players. Student managers were assigned the duty of waking Wendell up for classes. In college, if a player is talented enough, coaches will endure a few headaches.

To help navigate Wendell in a better direction, I gave him an assignment. I pulled him aside during one game and told him that Lawrence, our freshman big man, was having confidence issues. It wasn't true. But I told Wendell that he needed to encourage Lawrence, to give him reassurance that we were behind him. Wendell said he would take care of it. Suddenly, Wendell stopped worrying about the coaches on his butt and started caring about a teammate. I wasn't sure if it would work, but it did get Wendell out of his own way. When Lawrence played well, which was usually the case, I nodded to Wendell, insinuating that he had done a great job with Lawrence.

By giving such an assignment to other players, I could get them to stop worrying about themselves and instead think about the team. It didn't always work, but when it did, the entire team benefitted. I enjoyed moments like those when I knew I brought value to the team, even if the stats didn't show it or the fans and coaches didn't see it. Being a navigator had the same effect on me as it did the others: it made me stop focusing on my situation in favor of thinking about the team.

Being a cheerleader didn't usually bring recognition. A newspaper photo of me standing next to Coach Bliss showed us both pointing to something that apparently was important. I looked like his Mini-Me. Coach Bliss took time in film sessions to talk about being a complete team player, sometimes using me as an example. He told the team that even though I was no longer starting, I was making myself valuable. Coach recognizing me like that made me feel special.

DISAPPOINTING ENDING

Work hard, be patient, and be ready.

My philosophy again paid off. Two games later, I was back in the lineup for a stretch of games in which Coach started John and me. As the season wore on and John and I played together more, I came to know and understand him better. We experienced some great moments together on the court.

We hosted number twenty-two Missouri, and our fans packed the Ferrell Center in a way I hadn't seen since the Kansas upset the year before. Our game was on ESPN2 and the only game on national TV that night.

We gave our fans and the TV audience a great, tightly contested game. With thirty-nine seconds remaining, John made a huge three-pointer to put us ahead by one. Missouri answered with a quick basket to retake the lead with twenty-three seconds left. Most coaches call a timeout in that situation to set up a play, but Coach Bliss trusted us to go on our own. John dribbled down the left sideline toward me. I caught the pass with no option but to make something happen. I jabbed right and moved left, trying to get lower than the more athletic defender blanketing me. I saw two of Missouri's big guys also coming out toward me, so I launched into the air, hoping one would hit me. I drew contact, and the refs called the foul.

I stepped to the free throw line for two shots with eleven seconds on the clock.

I went through my routine and released the ball. I think the ball hit every part of the rim before going down. Coach Bliss jokingly told the media after the game, "I think it went in from the bottom." We were tied at 80. My second free throw was perfect. Missouri's Kareem Rush missed a last-second jumper, and we had defeated a top-twenty-five team to improve our conference record to 4–6.

Our team was young and still learning how to win in the Big 12, but John and I made a good combination on the floor. He provided the firepower, and I brought the calming influence. When John went rogue on offense, I intentionally tried to get the ball to Lawrence as much as possible. We had been building momentum, and the upset of Missouri injected a shot of excitement into our program.

I also had been drawing more media attention, including postgame interviews. I did not like talking about myself. John and I complemented each other that way, too, as he began filling the public talking role and I became the behind-the-scenes guy.

I had watched John work on his weak points throughout the season, but he still didn't get along with many people. I knew with him playing at such a high level and me starting games and logging more minutes, I needed to be his friend. We didn't have much in common, and we weren't going to be hanging out off the court, but our team needed me to be John's friend. "Baylor first, you second." And that is how I would keep my spot and my scholarship for another year.

We traveled to Kansas in mid-February as the regular season was winding down. The Jayhawks were ranked second in the nation. They also hadn't forgotten about us shocking them the year before in Waco. We arrived in Lawrence the day before the game and went to the historic Allen Fieldhouse for a night practice. We walked past students in lines of tents; they were camping out to get the best seats for the next day's game.

When we walked inside, I learned a lesson in work ethic. Nick Collison was one of my all-time favorite opponents at any level. He was the only player on the court, working with a coach on jumpers from the top of the key. Nick took each shot at game speed with total concentration. I had felt like I was playing in the big time seeing the students camping out for tickets. But inside, I learned from watching Nick how a big-time player works to perfect his game.

On game day, I saw yet another side of Coach Bliss. He was fifty-eight years old. After pregame warmups, as usual, we headed into the locker room. Coach was giving us our final prep when he unexpectedly stopped talking and looked at us. He looked twenty years younger. After his pause for effect, Coach said, "You guys know that feeling you have in your stomachs? That anticipation to play?" He looked directly into the eyes of players around the room. "I have that feeling too. Coaching, it's how I still compete."

Coach looked so thrilled to be in our locker room and so content with getting ready to compete with us that I felt a warmth in my heart. My coach was on the sideline caring just as much as we did about winning, about our effort, and about the product we put out on the floor!

We were twenty-two-point underdogs, but we managed to take a slight lead. Kansas being Kansas—especially playing at home—came back to take a four-point lead into halftime. We were disappointed we had lost our lead, and most of us were staring at nothing in particular when Coach slammed his fist into a metal locker.

"Do you realize the opportunity we have here?!?" he screamed, face reddened with intensity.

We were down only four points. We could still win at Allen Fieldhouse, which not many players can say they did during their careers. Wake-up call delivered, Coach calmly explained adjustments we would make in the second half. As he talked, I watched his hand tremble at his side. I was pretty sure he had broken a bone in there somewhere, and he had for sure left a dent in the locker door. A little questionable motivational tactic for sure, but I had to admire his passion as long as he was hitting something other than me.

We gave our best effort in the second half, but Kansas was just too tough for us. We lost by fifteen.

The Kansas loss was the second of six consecutive to end the conference schedule. We were the tenth seed for the Big 12 tournament and drew seventh-seeded Kansas State in the first round. We had defeated the Wildcats at home during the regular season, but our tournament matchup resembled much of our season. Our youth showed as K-State beat us in overtime.

We finished the season with a 14–16 record—a major disappointment and a step back from the excitement of playing in the NIT my freshman year. At least we had the pieces in place to build on. We would be much more experienced the next season, and I had two years left to attain my dream of playing in the NCAA Tournament.

6

SET FOR SUCCESS

Logan was the definition of a college student-athlete. He took care of business in the classroom and gave maximum effort on the court every day. But with Lawrence developing into an NBA-caliber player, Logan was in a similar situation to me playing behind John. There was one exception, though: with fewer spots on the floor for centers than guards, Logan had fewer avenues to finding playing time.

Logan told me late in the spring semester that he was transferring to Davidson College, where his brother had played. Davidson was looking for a big man like Logan, and he had been able to secure a spot on the team. Per NCAA transfer rules, he would have to sit out one season, but he would still have two years of eligibility remaining at a school that needed him.

The thought of saying goodbye to my friend and my roommate for two years hurt. I wanted to plead with Logan to stay because I believed we had a realistic chance to advance deep in the following postseason, and perhaps a better opportunity would develop for him. But Logan was a smart guy who came from a basketball family, and I knew he was making the best decision for himself. As Coach Bliss had made clear in his preseason speeches, college basketball was a business, and Logan made a business decision.

I stayed in Waco for the summer, as usual. Each day, I worked out hard, attended classes, and played sand volleyball. My weightlifting schedule was producing results, and my coaches and teammates noticed my increased strength.

Strength would be my equalizer. I routinely guarded larger players, like Kareem Rush from Missouri and Andre Emmett from Texas Tech. A more powerful, muscular frame would allow me to play more of a contact game on defense. I could slow down an opponent by staying in contact with him. In a one-on-one matchup, space creates an advantage for the quicker guy, and that wasn't me most of the time. Summer was my time to put in the work that would set me up to play more physically.

With Logan gone, I moved into a one-bedroom apartment. I had been following the progress of an abandoned church furniture factory's conversion into residential lofts. When the LL Sams Historic Lofts were ready for tenants, I moved into a sweet new home.

Being a D-I student-athlete came with perks. Picking up textbooks at the school bookstore was a lengthy, frustrating process for students. But not for athletes. I went into the bookstore to get books for my summer classes, and the checkout lines seemed to stretch out past Mars. Because I was on full scholarship, Baylor paid for my books. All I had to do was go to the front of the line, provide my name, and show my ID, and then I was handed bags of books with my name on them. The whole process took about two minutes. I could feel the eyes of the other students in line shooting laser beams into my back.

Food was another perk. Baylor had a program that allowed me to eat at a restaurant, sign my name, and not have to pay because the restaurant would bill the school. Technically, we were paying for the meals through our stipend, but the system made athletes feel like celebrities at times. Some let the special treatment go to their head. I understood the debates about whether athletes received too much preferential treatment, but I also appreciated my situation and tried to thank Baylor by representing the school and our program well.

In early August, Wendell, one of our most athletic players, was arrested for assault and possession of marijuana. When I heard, I shook my head in disbelief. Wendell had been arrested four months earlier for assaulting his girlfriend and burglary. He received deferred adjudication, and with Wendell coming up on his senior season, I was ready for his off-court troubles to be behind us. Considering Coach's desire to win, I wondered if he would only talk with Wendell and leave it at that.

Coach was in Europe, traveling with the Big 12 All-Stars. Every other year, the conference selected a head coach to lead an all-star team consisting of one player from each team. The all-stars spent about a week overseas playing games in different countries. To no one's surprise, Coach had selected Lawrence to represent our team. I hadn't followed how the all-stars were faring, but I assumed Coach would deal with Wendell when he returned.

I was correct. On August 26, Coach dismissed Wendell from the team, making this statement: "We wish Wendell well. We tried to understand and work with Wendell. We think a new start in another location would be best for him." When I heard that, I thought the location Coach Bliss meant was jail.

I hated to see Wendell go because he was a gifted athlete with excellent basketball skills. He had more athleticism in his pinky than I had in my whole body. Wendell was one of those guys for whom things had always seemed to come easily, and it wound up hurting him. The amount of extra time Coach spent dealing with Wendell was a distraction. It was difficult for hard-working role players like me to see Wendell skip weights with no punishment. Wendell's departure was another example of what I had seen and heard of countless times: players quit, transfer, get injured, land in the coach's doghouse, and, in extreme cases, get dismissed from the team. Yet, life always seemed to roll on in college athletics.

My biggest issue of the summer was dealing with a shoulder injury. Coach Bliss selected me to play for a team of all-stars that played six games in London against local pro teams. I felt honored that he chose me, and when I learned that I would be a starter, I chalked up the news as proof that all my hard work was paying off. Our team's coach was Taylor "Tates" Locke, a well-known former college coach and NBA scout. He gave me a confidence boost when he instantly expressed his approval of my aggressive, hard-nosed style of play.

The trip was remarkable except for one moment. I was cutting full speed through the paint when a 300-pound English player slammed my right shoulder, knocking me to the ground. I hopped up, sprinted toward the other end, and drew a charge on defense. As I got up from the floor after that contact, my right arm wouldn't move. Trainers diagnosed a separated shoulder.

Back home at Baylor, our team trainer gave me two choices: surgery or receive a shot and play through it. Surgery would have meant eight to ten weeks of recovery. A player like me couldn't afford to miss any time. Easy choice! Within ten minutes of receiving the shot, I could do pushups and shoot like nothing had happened.

Coach Bliss was beaming when practices began in October. Because our teams had improved under him, attendance at home games had increased. More fans meant more money, which paid for a brand new air-cushioned court at the Ferrell Center and a large video board overheard.

The Big 12 coaches had picked us to finish eighth in the conference, but other preseason polls placed us sixth because our arena wasn't the only part of our program that featured upgrades.

I really liked our new roster. The three freshmen studs from last season now had the experience gained from their first go-round in the Big 12. The sophomore role players, including me, now were upperclassmen. We knew more of what to expect this season. And Coach Bliss and his assistants had signed four junior college (juco) transfers—Terrance Thomas, Ellis Kidd, Robert Hart, and Carlton "Dottie" Dotson—who brought us the depth we had sorely lacked. We also had six-ten R.T. Guinn available after sitting out the previous season following his transfer from New Mexico.

Good coaches use every tool available to them, and inside the locker room, I noticed Coach Bliss had assigned me the locker between John and Lawrence. My sophomore year, I had encouraged Lawrence when he was frustrated about a loss or playing poorly. John, on the other hand, was a firecracker. My intent with him was to keep him focused on the team instead of himself. Based on my locker location, I had no doubt I would be continuing in my role as team navigator.

I couldn't help but feel we were embarking on a special season. I was more confident in myself because, after the roller coaster of moving in and out of the starting lineup the year before, I understood how to weather a college season. I expected our new players would impress Coach Bliss early on, and he would give them more opportunities than me. But Coach knew me and what I contributed to the team. I was determined to be a great teammate and always be supportive. Other players would experience their highs and lows, but I would be consistent. And when Coach Bliss inevitably turned to me, I would be ready just as I had the previous two seasons.

CLASHING PERSONALITIES

We encountered adversity before our first game arrived. Lawrence suffered a stress fracture in his left leg that would keep him out the first five weeks of the season. Terrance, a six-six guard who could handle, pass, and score, reported out of shape. "Tall T" and I had played on a select team in Dallas together, and I was excited when he transferred in from Lon Morris Junior College. I expected him to contribute right away before he got off to a bad start with Coach Bliss. John's issues with Coach his freshman year were nothing compared to Terrance's. Terrance seemed upset about everything.

We won our first four games before falling to TCU. R.T. was a pleasant early surprise with solid shooting. Carlos, another of our juco transfers, figured to be a great fit in our flex offense because he was a six-eight power forward with a nice outside shot. But Dottie was still trying to learn our system. Terrance also was struggling on the court in addition to going toe-to-toe with Coach Bliss.

The relationship between Coach and Terrance was distractingly awkward at times. During a scrimmage in practice, Terrance took a questionable shot. Coach brought practice to a screaming stop. Neck muscles bulging and face bright red, he pointed at Terrance and told him how bad of a shot that was, employing descriptive language to which I had become not entirely accustomed. We could tell Terrance did not like being singled out in front of the team.

We resumed the scrimmage, and a few minutes later, a shot similar to Terrance's opened for me. I took it. Coach Bliss said nothing about my shot selection.

"Why don't you yell at him?" Terrance shouted at Coach Bliss.

Lawrence stepped in and told me, "You keep taking that shot. It's a good one."

Terrance was stewing.

What bothered me most about Terrance's attitude was how he didn't appear to want to be on the team that I loved. The adjustment from junior college to D-I could be difficult because the style of play at the juco level tended to resemble organized pickup. Junior-college ball was all about shot selection and how fast players could score. The defensive intensity was drastically less. The transition to a controlled, high-pressure style at our level—especially under a coach as controlling as Coach Bliss—could understandably be confusing. I had kind of assumed that Terrance wouldn't make it to even the first game, and now I didn't see how he could make it through the rest of the scrimmage.

Patrick Dennehy also presented a team chemistry problem. He was redshirting in order to extend his eligibility, and as a power forward who seemed destined for the NBA, he could be valuable in practice to prepare us for some big opponents. Except Patrick had his quirks. His confidence sometimes turned into cockiness, and he had an air about him that shouted, "I am Patrick Dennehy, and you guys get out of the way." Patrick didn't always mesh well with the rest of the team. As I tried to get to know him, I found him to be aloof and socially awkward. Over time, I was able to get closer to him and see that he was a nice guy—very friendly, just different.

I could already see an interesting situation brewing. Patrick had unlimited potential. I think everybody on the team knew that the next season, after Patrick had completed his redshirt, he would be taking Dottie's starting spot. They were roommates, and that was going to be a delicate situation.

Dottie, on the other hand, was great in practice. He was a tough competitor who didn't back down from confrontations. Dottie and I got along great. At times, we would both be on the bench cheering on our teammates. I rooted for Dottie to improve his game because he could be easier to get along with than Patrick.

As the nonconference season progressed, I replaced Terrance whenever he wasn't playing well. There was always an awkward tension when I subbed in for T. I felt like apologizing to him and blaming Coach Bliss for putting me in. Practices still were regularly interrupted by Terrance and Coach engaging in crazy shouting matches. Coach kicked him out of one practice. I went back and forth predicting which would happen first: Coach would dismiss him from the team or Terrance would quit.

We weren't exchanging many Christmas gifts in the locker room, but we were in the business of winning, and we were taking care of business. We ended nonconference play with a 9–2 record.

PAYING THE PRICE

I turned twenty-one in January having never tasted alcohol. A few of our relatives had drinking problems, and my mom had warned my sister and me about the dangers. I was paranoid about alcohol affecting my basketball career. To celebrate my twenty-first birthday, I drank two bottles of Mike's Hard Lemonade because it sounded like a normal drink. Yet part of me was terrified of what even that 5 percent alcohol would do to my body. *Would I immediately get drunk or hooked? Would it affect my play?* I remembered the story of Samson and how he lost his strength when he compromised his values. *Would trying alcohol cause me to lose God's blessing on my life?*

I did recognize that I was living a charmed life. I was competing at a higher level of basketball than might be expected for someone with my build and ability. Both parents were still in my life, and they were very supportive. Other than the shoulder injury, I had suffered only minor aches and pains in my first two seasons. And that's with a reckless style of play that had me diving for loose balls. I had a public goal of breaking at least one of the advertisement boards along the sideline scorer's table before I graduated. If a ball headed toward the boards in games or practice, I was on it. Sometimes in practice, coaches or managers intentionally threw a ball into the sideboards to see if I could get it.

I also prided myself in setting screens and taking charges, refusing to back down to bigger guys who often barreled over me. I defended players who had fifty to seventy pounds on me. Getting tossed around added to the nicks and dings.

Part of the reason I was getting onto the floor so much was my willingness to literally do just that, but that style of play was taking its toll.

My first ongoing injury was in my neck. Constant shooting pain traveled down each arm to my fingertips, and I could not move my neck, much less play basketball. The coaches brought in a chiropractor, but he couldn't help me. I was diagnosed with a slight disc bulge at the base of my neck. Through trial and error, I found that combining an energy drink and pain medication before a game or during halftime made the pain tolerable. That was the only way I could play, and I knew that if I sat out for any length of time to give my neck time to heal, I was not talented enough to come back. I decided I would do whatever it took to continue playing.

We lost our first six conference games before defeating Texas A&M at home. We couldn't seem to get everyone playing well at the same time.

Lawrence was back from his injury, and he and John were lighting it up. Kenny was playing well. R.T. was starting, and Ellis was starting ahead of me. But Dottie was struggling, and his minutes had dwindled. I noticed his attitude changing for the worse. I felt for him because I knew what it was like to get buried on the bench and lose hope. Terrance was also struggling, and his attitude was not good. I was amazed he still was on the team.

Practices could be odd. Patrick often missed practice, and none of us knew where he was or why he didn't show. Sometimes, he popped in and showed us his newest tattoo or piercing. As a redshirt, Patrick was assigned to the scout team when he did show and did a good job preparing us for the next opponent's best big player. But no one knew when he would come to practice.

Coach Bliss mostly filled the scout team with walk-ons, redshirts, and any player currently in his doghouse. Occasionally, he assigned me to the scout team, which was also called the white team because that was the color of its jerseys. Coach focused on working with the green squad to prepare those players for the next game. Being on the white team bothered me because I knew the coaches weren't looking at us or concerned with coaching us. When Coach Bliss put me on the scout team, he would usually tell me something like, "Matt, I know you know this stuff, so I am going to have you work with the white squad today." I always answered respectfully, "Yes, sir." I couldn't let Coach see how much it bothered me to be stuck on the scout team.

After defeating A&M to end our losing streak, we played at Oklahoma. We lost by forty-nine points. Afterward, our heads were hanging in embarrassment, but Coach was relatively calm. Perhaps he had had most of the game to accept we were getting clobbered. But I was still on alert for one of his fits of rage.

Suddenly, Coach snapped his fingers and turned to Steve Raquet, a hard-working walk-on. "I should have gotten you into the game," he said.

I thought, *That takes a lot of class to admit you made a mistake and also to acknowledge Steve's hard work at practice.*

"Why didn't you?" Terrance asked Coach defiantly.

Total silence.

I slowly raised my head. In my three years at Baylor, no one had ever addressed Coach like that, and I wouldn't dare miss Coach's response. I pictured the chalk outline around Terrance's body.

Coach Bliss turned and glared right at T. We were waiting for it. Then, nothing. Coach turned and walked away. Perhaps he knew he was wrong. Somehow, once again, Terrance had lasted another day.

Kansas beat us by twenty-one at home in our next game, and then we traveled to Stillwater, Oklahoma, to play thirteenth-ranked Oklahoma State and legendary coach Eddie Sutton. At one point in the season, six teams from our conference held spots in the national top twenty-five. I loved that on any given night, I could play against the best teams in the country.

Leading up to the game, I dealt with pain throbbing from my neck down both arms and through my fingertips. I was unable to turn my head. But Coach had inserted me into the starting lineup alongside John, and I wasn't giving up my starting position.

In Stillwater, Coach let me sit in the hot tub and then sleep during the game day walkthrough. I was on so much pain medication that I felt like I was in a dream. Trainers said they would place a heating pad on my neck each time I subbed out during the game.

Coach took a different approach for this game, telling us to run like we had never run before. The up-tempo strategy worked; from the opening tip, Oklahoma State had no way to stop John. We led by as many as fifteen points in the first half and took a twelve-point lead into halftime. We pushed the lead back to fifteen in the second half. But playing like a team that had beaten us eleven times in a row—which they had—the Cowboys came charging back to take a five-point lead with just under five minutes to play. But this time, we got 'em. We clamped down defensively, Kenny hit a big three-pointer late, and we won 74–72. We were only 2–8 in conference play, but in ending Oklahoma State's seventeen-game home winning streak, we proved to ourselves that we were capable of beating anyone in the league.

YEARNING FOR MORE

In early March, Coach took me to another FCA event. Following the usual routine, I talked about my faith and the importance of prayer. I added a bit about playing basketball and turned the program over to Coach Bliss. Like all the previous times, he was patterned and organized in nailing his speech. As I listened this time, I realized that after three years with Coach, I knew little about him. I didn't know what he liked or disliked or if he had any hobbies. Even his speeches revealed little about him. He was a guarded man. He was all business.

A few days later, I dropped something off in Coach's office. He was dissecting game tape, an ability for which he had no equal. He looked up from the film and said, "Matt, look at this." He played a clip of me reading my defender's movement on a screen and slipping past to score. Smiling, he said, "Only you could've seen that." I wished I'd had more little, personal moments like that with him, but they were few and far between.

Coach Bliss was a bipolar type of person. On his positive side, he talked about prayer and his religious beliefs. He shared sayings like, "The thing about a man is having pride in what you do" or "The thing about a man is having integrity." He seemed to care about the development of his players. When he complimented my play in his office, he seemed genuine. When he told Steve that he should have played him in the University of Oklahoma (OU) game, I believed he meant it.

On the negative side, Coach had emotional outbursts that weren't just coaching ploys to deliver a message. He visibly became thoroughly enraged, like a demon was inside and wanting to come out. He spent so much energy on his carefully crafted image that once the fuse was lit, he could not prevent the explosion. I couldn't imagine the pressure he felt. He was being paid an incredible amount of money to turn our program around, a task he had accomplished multiple times. But his success also brought unbelievable expectations.

As a people-pleaser, I learned to be whatever Coach wanted me to be. Baylor first, you second—that was me. I recognized how coaching worked. College players came with the basic skill set to play the game. Coaches like Bliss were fine-tuners who would remind players of the concepts and techniques they already knew and crack down on the players when they slipped up. Coaches must be master managers and manipulators, able to trick players with egos and selfish ambitions into caring more about the team than themselves. Coach Bliss's track record showed he knew what he was doing. Still, I thought about his contrasting personalities, and I wondered when he would teach me golf like he told my mother he would. Perhaps that would happen my senior year, and I would get to know him personally on the golf course.

THE BEST IS YET TO COME

The Oklahoma State victory started a three-game winning streak.... which was followed by a three-game losing streak leading into our final game of the regular season, at home against Coach Bobby Knight's Texas Tech Red Raiders. Coach Bliss knew Coach Knight backward and forward, and he laid out a brilliant game plan. First, he assigned our least athletic starter—me—to cover Tech's most athletic player, Andre Emmett. Emmett had an amazing post-up game with a wicked spin move, but Coach believed I could defend him because I was strong enough, tough enough, and intelligent enough to anticipate a "tell" Emmett had that tipped off his next move. Although Tech had decent shooters, Coach Knight rarely allowed three-point shots. He designed his motion offense to attack the basket. Coach Bliss instructed us to make sure that at all times, in every Tech possession, at least three of us were defending in the paint.

Coach had us incredibly prepared for success throughout the season, but as our 13–13 record indicated, we struggled to execute late in close games. Our inability to finish off games we should have won was becoming increasingly frustrating. On this night, though, we executed Coach Bliss's game plan for a 74–68 win.

We entered the Big 12 tournament as the tenth seed, far below the preseason predictions. But the Oklahoma State road win and the defeat of Tech at home gave us confidence that we could still play to our potential and reach either the NCAA Tournament or the NIT. I actually loved our possibilities, and I could tell Coach Bliss did too.

That season's conference tournament was at American Airlines Center in Dallas. The home of the Dallas Mavericks was just 100 miles from Baylor, meaning more of our fans could attend. It also was only a half-hour's drive from The Colony, so many of my friends and former coaches would be able to see me play.

We drew number seven seed Texas Tech in the first round. I was confident that with our strategy from the previous game, we could unleash our offense on Tech and put them away in a manner that would allow us to limit starters' minutes and rest them for the remainder of the tournament when we played teams that had earned first-round byes.

The starting lineup posted in the locker room shocked me. John and I weren't together. My number was on the board, but Andrew White's number 12 was in John's place. John had been butting heads with Coach again and was keeping Terrance company in the doghouse. Andrew was a senior walk-on and a high-character guy who had worked tirelessly for four years with little recognition.

We started strong, with inspiring play from Andrew. Tech wasn't guarding me closely because I had been a facilitator more than a scorer during the regular season. But in this game, I felt an urgency to make plays, and I knocked down two open shots early. I also guarded Emmett again. At six-five and weighing 240 pounds, his size advantage was obvious. But all my time watching film and preparing physically gave me the ability to compete against him.

After leading 36–32 at halftime, we showed signs of pulling away, but Tech stayed within reach of us. With 2:12 left, I was fouled and headed to the line for a one-and-one. For the season, I was 14-for-14 at the free throw line in the last three minutes of games. As the ref tossed me the ball, two odd things occupied my mind. First, I realized I had yet to shoot a free throw in this game. Second, earlier in the game, Emmett had accidentally kneed me in the thigh, giving me a painful "dead leg." Now, standing at the free throw line, my legs felt off-balance. I don't know why I allowed those negative thoughts to enter my mind in that crucial moment, but I missed the first free throw attempt. Tech scored quickly to cut our lead to one, and I was fouled again. I yelled, "Let's go!" after the ref's call. I had been in this position numerous times during my career and had been successful. There was no way I would miss again. I missed the front end of another one-and-one. Emmett scored with 12.4

seconds left to put Tech up 66–65, and John missed a tough shot for the lead. We had to foul, and Tech made both free throws for the final three-point margin.

My junior season had come to an end, and before I had left the court, I blamed myself for this loss. The team needed me to come through in clutch time, and I had failed.

Back at the team hotel, Coach Bliss and I wound up alone in an elevator. I had let my mentor down, and I could barely lift my head to look at him.

"I am sorry, Coach."

Coach stood straight up and looked into my eyes.

"There is no one else I want shooting those free throws more than you," he told me.

Sunlight peeked through the elevator doors.

Coaches like Bliss can yell, say hurtful words, and do crazy things. But if they validate a player's effort and what he does, the player will follow his coach through walls of fire if asked. That's how I felt about Coach Bliss.

Despite the disappointment of a 14–14 season, I carried a lot of optimism about the program and the next season. Lawrence, John, and Kenny—our three leading scorers—were returning with two solid years of experience. The crazy-talented Patrick would be eligible. Tyrone Nelson, a top recruit as a six-ten center, was coming in. So was Harvey Thomas, a top juco player. Our coaches were stacking up the talent.

I had played eighty-nine games over my three seasons. The payoff was coming for all the hard work, fighting through the injuries, seeing better players starting ahead of me, accepting my changing roles, and everything else I had faced. Coach Bliss was now twelfth among active coaches with over 500 career victories. He knew the formula for success, and he had started implementing it three years earlier while I was part of his first Baylor recruiting class. We were establishing the foundation for years of Baylor teams to build on, and my senior year would be the best ever. I was truly blessed. I went into the offseason believing nothing could stop me from the success for which I had worked so hard.

My last summer at Baylor started much like the previous ones. Classes in the morning, then a hard workout in the Ferrell Center. Maybe lunch at one of the preferred area restaurants followed by sand volleyball in the bright sun. The most significant difference from the previous summers was that this one included an elevated amount of energy and excitement for the coming season, my final one as a Bear. I couldn't wait.

So, it was no big deal when an assistant coach came into the weight room on a Friday and informed us of a team meeting after our workout. We met less frequently during the summer but still regularly.

As I hit it hard in the weight room, I imagined Coach Bliss pulling out another of his inspirational speeches designed to push us to keep working hard and reach our goals.

Headphones on, I continued lifting. Nothing seemed out of the ordinary.

7

THE LONGEST SUMMER BEGINS

After those of us who had stayed for the summer assembled, the first sign that this team meeting was not just like any other came when a police officer was the first to enter the room. Then a second officer came in. Their expressions were grim and serious. We straightened up in our seats and exchanged curious glances.

Who had done something wrong? And where was Coach Bliss?

Then Coach appeared, quickly said, "These officers need to ask you some questions," and stepped aside.

The lead officer cleared his throat and said the Waco Police Department was investigating Patrick Dennehy's whereabouts. His parents had not heard from him in two weeks, the officer said, and then asked if any of us had recently seen him. It was June 20, and Patrick had been in and out since the semester ended, the same as during the season.

Patrick had a new roommate, who I did not know. Patrick had been living with Dottie until, from what I understood, Dottie and his wife started divorce proceedings in April.

Dottie had replaced Logan on the court, but he was hit with the harsh truth that college athletics could be a business with little loyalty. He was released from the team postseason. Just as the other players and I had suspected, Patrick was filling Dottie's slot on the team now that his redshirt year was over.

No one in the locker room acknowledged seeing Patrick lately or knowing where he was. The officer told us they had talked with Patrick's roommate, and he did not know Patrick's whereabouts either. The roommate had returned home and found that Patrick's dogs had not been fed for several days. He relayed that information to Patrick's parents. Considering that Patrick had not called home on Father's Day, his parents filed a missing person's report.

As the officer appeared to be wrapping up his questions, I looked over at Coach Bliss to try to read his mood. He wasn't offering much to go on. I decided this was not a big deal and that Patrick probably was off somewhere having fun. After all, with Wendell's arrests and other players getting into trouble, we had seen crazier things happen than a teammate go off for a week of partying without communicating to anyone. The cost of being a good D-I program is occasional drama.

After we were dismissed, the officers remained in the room to talk with Coach Bliss. Within an hour, I was playing volleyball, taking care of my business of preparing for the upcoming season.

The following Friday, I received the phone call from Professor Browning alerting me of the local TV reports. I switched back and forth between the local stations, trembling, nauseated from reports that Waco PD was treating Patrick's absence as a possible homicide.

But then again, this was Patrick. He was different than everybody else—a character. At any moment, he could walk in and show off his newest tattoo or piercing. Over the next couple of hours, as I watched report after report, my optimism waned. It seemed like the police knew more than they released to the public. I believed they were on to something. On to some*one*.

I needed sound advice. My father was always the first person I'd call in confusing situations, and he would make sense of this mess for me.

Dad was watching the news in Dallas.

"What do you think will happen?" I asked.

Dad hesitated, drawing in a deep breath.

"Well, this is bad," he said. "I'm not sure Bliss is going to survive this." Without hesitating, he added, "And you might not have a program next year."

His next words sucked the last remaining hopes I held that, somehow, this situation would turn out to not be a big deal after all.

"You might want to think about looking somewhere else," Dad told me.

"What?" I asked. "Why would Coach Bliss be gone? And our program? That's not possible!"

I calmed down and reasoned that if someone murdered Patrick, as tragic as that would be, there was no reason Coach Bliss could be responsible. Baylor would not shut down our program because a player died. And besides, Patrick was going to make idiots out of everyone when he showed up with his latest body mod.

I hadn't experienced many low points in my life, but when I had, my remedy was to look forward to the next season. In this case, I was staring into the possibility of an uncertain season along with a teammate being dead. Basketball couldn't provide the escape this time because basketball was the problem.

Mom had taught me to try my best and rely on God for the rest. But what if this situation was too big for God? What could I do?

Since turning twenty-one, I had a few drinks now and then. I didn't want to drink until I felt out of control, though, because I had seen people do stupid things when they weren't thinking clearly. Drinking was merely a social activity for me. I was in college, and it was legal. But this night, I didn't want to think clearly. I wanted to erase the past few hours and the next few too. Maybe I would wake up and learn everything was just a big mistake. Who could blame me? It was Friday night, and other students were out having a good time. I needed to feel good for a short while. To take a timeout from life.

I woke up Saturday morning with my head pounding. The scary realization was that although I was suffering the consequences now, my decision the night before had worked. For a few hours, I had forgotten about everything going on. I was released from the stress and pressure. I was able to laugh, even if only temporarily.

My cell phone buzzed on the dresser. It had been ringing almost nonstop with calls from friends and the media, all wanting me to tell them something only I, as a player, could know. I told each one the truth: I didn't know anything they didn't know. When I grew tired of answering the phone, I let calls go to voicemail to screen them.

I dragged myself and my headache to the corner gas station to buy a protein drink and ibuprofen. I stopped to scan the *Waco Tribune-Herald* headlines. The front page said police were investigating possible threats made to Patrick by other players.

Other players? Was I one considered of those "other players"?

Subtract Dottie and the seniors who had graduated, and we had only about ten "other players." Until doing the math, I had not considered that I could be that involved in this story.

The story also detailed how Patrick's Chevy Tahoe had been found by police on June 25 in Virginia Beach, Virginia. The license plates had been removed. Continuing to hold on to any thread of hope and praying this would all turn out well, I thought of the possibility that Patrick's plates had fallen off and he was living it up in Virginia. But the hopeful thoughts couldn't last long when new information surfaced at lightning speed.

That afternoon, Coach Bliss released a statement that read in part, "Right now the team, the university, all the members of the Baylor family and myself are just in disbelief about these latest reports. In fact, no part of it seems real. To everyone listening, I would like to ask you to help us—help us pray, and help us understand. Our thoughts and prayers are with Patrick's family and loved ones."

I assumed Coach had help crafting the statement, but it was well done. He touched on the feelings and emotions I was experiencing. I didn't believe my dad's prediction could be correct. Coach Bliss would lead us out of this dark time.

The deluge of phone calls the rest of the day wore me out. My world was slowly turning upside down, and I could not make sense of it.

NOTHING BUT QUESTIONS

With each day, the news had been growing worse. But Sunday morning, as was the case every day, I couldn't stop myself from grabbing the newspapers.

One article said police had followed up on leads and believed Patrick's murder occurred in the Waco area. Then came the shocker from Waco police spokesman Steven Anderson: "From that lead and a few others, potential suspects in the disappearance of Dennehy potentially include fellow Baylor basketball players."

Who on our team would want to kill Patrick? And why?

I needed to get dressed for church, where I could seek guidance from the Lord and hang out with people who would lead me in the right direction. I received a call from a police department secretary informing me that I needed to go to the police station at 8 a.m. Monday morning and provide a statement. My heart started running wind sprints when she said, "They have some questions for you."

I had nothing to do with Patrick's disappearance. I knew nothing. But what if the police mistakenly believed I was involved? My palms were clammy as I ended the call.

I didn't want to think about the next morning's interview, and I knew of only one activity that would distract me. A few of my teammates who had remained in town were more than eager to join me at Cricket's Grill and Draft House. Because it was Sunday night, I figured the place wouldn't be too busy, and we could have fun without worrying about who might be watching. Besides, I deserved a few hours of peace.

Growing up, what I heard about alcohol made it seem like drinking was from the devil. But I found comfort sitting with the few people who understood what I was feeling. With every drink I took, my fears over my teammate's life and my basketball uncertainty shifted more and more into the distance. It was scary how this newfound means of distraction seemed to be working.

Monday morning, my alarm sent a deep spike of pain through my head. I rubbed my head, thinking I must have hit something the night before. No bump, just a lot of ache, although I found a bruise on my arm that I later learned was the result of falling down a flight of stairs.

It was 7 o'clock. I reached for the snooze button and vaguely remembered there was something I needed to do that morning. Even a place I was supposed to go. *But where?* I tried willing my brain to focus, but it didn't work. I rolled over to my left, and it hit me.

The police interview!

I raced toward the shower, bashing my foot on the dresser. I hurried to get ready, continuing to bump into things. I wasn't so sure that the previous night's activities were worth this. And in less than an hour, I would be questioned about my teammate's possible murder. I needed to get my act together.

This was my first trip to a police station. It was already hot outside when I arrived, and I was sweating before getting out of the car. The building's exterior didn't seem so frightening. That feeling changed as soon as I walked inside. I went up to the front desk and gave my name. Within a few minutes, a detective came, introduced himself, and escorted me to an interview room.

The interview room was not like any I had seen on TV shows. The office had a desk with chairs on opposite sides. There was no one-way glass. It looked like a regular office, but that didn't make it less terrifying. Plus, I was afraid of what might happen if the detective noticed my hangover.

The detective casually dropped his folder with a notepad onto the table. He said he would be asking me some questions. His demeanor suggested this was no big deal, but I don't recall him offering any reassuring words before the questions began.

"Did you hang out with Patrick?"

"Had you heard any rumors of players not liking each other?"

"How well did you know Patrick?"

"Had you noticed anything strange?"

"When did you last talk to Patrick?"

"How well do you know Carlton?"

My brain was not up to speed yet, and it took a lot of effort to answer the best I could.

The detective wanted more details, and his questions started to become repetitive. I tried to give him what he wanted. Then, finally, he placed a sheet of paper in front of me and asked me to write out a statement. I nodded because I wanted out of there. The truth was that I hadn't involved myself with my teammates outside of basketball. I knew little about their party habits and girl dramas. I caught a glimpse of how much trouble I had avoided because of how I lived. After I signed my name at the bottom of the statement, the detective escorted me out.

Back outside, I wiped my sweaty hands on my khakis as I fumbled with the car keys. My mouth was dry, so I tried to lick my lips. But my tongue produced no saliva. Mostly, I was annoyed. Where was Patrick? A teammate disappearing wasn't in my plan. We were supposed to be focusing on basketball and winning!

All of a sudden, I felt like I could really use a drink. I was still a novice at drinking and wondered whether 10 a.m. was too early to start. I decided I should wait.

I pulled into a Kwik Stop to get gas. Outside the front door, the row of newspaper vending machines stared at me. *USA Today. Waco Tribune-Herald. The Dallas Morning News.* All screamed headlines with the words "Murder," "Baylor," and "Basketball." I could not stop looking at the nasty headlines and the news beneath them.

The police had unsealed an affidavit that mentioned a search of Patrick's computer. It also revealed an informant in Delaware told police Dottie had told a cousin that he had shot and killed Patrick during an argument while they were firing guns in Waco. Dottie had returned home to Hurlock, Maryland, and was being sought for questioning. He was considered a "person of interest."

Out of the corner of my eye, I noticed two people, a girl and a guy, staring at me. I was accustomed to people in Waco recognizing me. Unlike a college football team, which can have up to 125 active players, there are only fifteen players for basketball, so there aren't that many guys to know. Plus, I stood out as one of Baylor's few white players. Most times when I was recognized, I would see people mouth the words "basketball player" to each other. But these two had a different look, as if I had done something wrong or perhaps even committed a

THE LONGEST SUMMER BEGINS   109

crime. I wanted to tell them, "First of all, I'm learning about this right along with you here." But I said nothing.

The next several days limped along. I tried to stay in my daily routine, but it was nearly impossible to concentrate. The Ferrell Center was a ghost town. Anyone I saw there—coaches, players, employees—nodded to each other without saying much. When I went to the SLC to work out or play hoops, awkward gazes greeted me. The campus I loved was closing in on me. My desire to work on my game and improve for next season almost disappeared. *Next season? What future was there now?* I felt like I could do nothing to change my course. I was simply along for the ride now.

Only a handful of players and a few walk-ons remained on campus. John, Lawrence, and Kenny had escaped to Houston. My phone continued to ring with reporters in search of answers I could not provide. They were asking many of the same questions I had. I answered and returned as many calls as I could.

Each day, the questions grew progressively worse.

"Is Dennehy dead?"

"Do you know of anyone who would want him dead?"

"Tell us all you know about Dottie."

The media had become a monster needing its daily feeding.

More and more, I found myself retreating into my apartment to be alone. I completely neglected what I had grown up knowing and believing: that God has a plan for all of us. I also knew that Christians weren't exempt from bad things happening to them. But I had believed that I lived such a blessed life because I stayed out of trouble. Now, this situation did not make sense.

Disbelief began festering inside of me. I could think of only one solution. I had to numb it all.

8

THE HITS KEEP COMING

What should have been another fun summer in Waco was anything but. The days crept by, and I hid in my apartment as much as I could. I woke up in the mornings struggling to remember the end to the previous night's ventures.

Skipping class didn't bother me, and when I did attend, I showed up late and slipped into the back of the classroom. I wore a ball cap and looked down to avoid eye contact. Around Waco, I hoped no one recognized me. I still couldn't help looking at newspaper headlines even though I knew they would ruin my day.

Coach Bliss scheduled a news conference for Thursday, July 10. Dottie appeared to be emerging as the prime suspect, and Patrick still had not been located. Hopefully, Coach had information to pass on. With his ability to control a room, Coach could make everyone feel better. When I saw only a small group of reporters standing in our locker room, I was encouraged that the story might finally be on its last legs.

Coach stood a few feet from Patrick's empty locker as he spoke.

First, he talked about his prayers and concerns for Patrick's family. Then he said he was in uncharted territory as a coach because he had no experience with such a nightmare. However, he added, he was the captain in charge of steering our ship through these rough waters.

I needed to hear that we had a captain who wasn't running from his duties. For a Baylor first, me second guy, I was struck by how selfish I had become, focusing on how my plans were impacted. I could not imagine what Patrick's family was going through, the fear and rage they must be feeling. And Dottie's family had to be going crazy wondering what would happen to their son. *Was he capable of what he was suspected of doing?* Thinking about those two families made me ashamed of the "me monster" growing inside me. Until recently, I had always cared more about others than myself.

When a reporter asked whether Coach Bliss and his staff had done all they could to locate Patrick and keep tabs on players in their program, Coach seemed ready with an answer. He explained that Patrick had missed class on June 16, and the coaches were concerned not because they thought something had happened to him at that point but because he needed to complete that class to be academically eligible. One of his staff members called Patrick's mother, but all they had was a work number at a place where she was no longer employed. Coach Bliss said his coaches became more urgent and contacted several people who might know where Patrick was. They learned that Patrick had said he was going to Arlington, Texas, over the weekend to visit friends, so they assumed he had stayed longer and missed class on Monday. But when he wasn't in class on Tuesday, they ramped up their search. I noticed that Coach did not tell reporters about our team meeting with the police.

To me, it sounded like our coaches' actions were what any other college coaches would have done regarding an athlete close to becoming ineligible.

Coach Bliss then shifted to talking about how our team was dealing with the situation. He said Patrick was like a son to him and like a brother to his teammates. He said counseling had been prepared for us, and that he was still holding out hope for a good outcome.

I needed to hear that the captain still believed everything could turn out okay.

Then Coach Bliss added that he did not believe one of his current players was involved in Patrick's disappearance. The word "current" jumped out at me. Dottie was no longer a current member of the team. Coach refuted rumors that the coaching staff knew of any threats to Patrick or Dottie. Dottie had recently had some money stolen, and Patrick's car was broken into. The coaches told both to contact the police and make a report.

Coach concluded by describing how the coaching staff was still recruiting as usual. He detailed the camps he was running and campus visits he was handling. In that regard, the coaches were going through a routine summer. For a change, I felt normal too. This would all blow over soon, and Patrick would show up.

Everything *was* going to be all right.

FEARS COME TRUE

I had begun to dread Mondays because of how my body revolted over my weekend festivities. I started this Monday sluggish, unmotivated, and flat-out miserable. I had zero desire to hit the gym and prepare for next season, if there would be one. I was realizing that no matter how much I had tried to escape the night before, today's problems would be unmerciful. I couldn't understand why I was doing this to myself.

I turned on the TV to a station teasing more breaking news. I sat on my couch, wondering what the breaking news could be this time. As I waited, I thought back on the most recent developments and whether they indicated what was to come.

Three days earlier, Dottie had contacted a sheriff's department in Maryland and said he wanted to talk. If the sheriff's department had anything on Dottie, I assumed, they would have arrested him instead of allowing him to return home. The next day, a man mowing at a Waco apartment complex had found a 9mm handgun in a plastic bag. The police said they were examining the gun for clues. Patrick's girlfriend told police that Harvey Thomas, our new juco transfer, lived at that complex. According to an affidavit she filed, Patrick had talked about being threatened by someone named Harvey. Patrick had been Harvey's host on his first Baylor visit. Patrick introduced Harvey to Dottie, and the three of them ran around together. The affidavit also said that following the threats, Patrick had changed his locks and, along with Dottie, started answering the door with a handgun ready. Coach Bliss had denied any involvement by Harvey, but adding a new teammate to the list of suspects twisted the situation into knots.

Then on that Sunday, Jeff Miller of *The Dallas Morning News* reported that during a telephone interview the previous day, Dottie had said Baylor had treated him unfairly and unjustly. According to the article, Dottie said little else. I assumed Dottie was upset about losing his scholarship.

Then the TV station delivered the breaking news: Dottie had been arrested in Maryland and charged with murdering Patrick. Dottie was in jail awaiting transfer to Waco. Even though Patrick's body had not been found, authorities were confident he was dead. Dottie reportedly had checked himself into a hospital, claiming he was delusional. After Dottie left the hospital, he confessed to killing Patrick.

We had dealt with this story for a month, but hearing that Patrick was believed dead was tough to accept. I felt horrible for his parents, who would never enjoy the pleasure my parents did of seeing their son play in a Baylor uniform. I thought of the many times I had sat by Dottie on the bench, of all the conversations I'd had with someone I would never have believed capable of taking Patrick's life. And hearing what we had feared could be true, I also couldn't help but selfishly wonder about our team's future. About my future. Had Baylor basketball reached its peak?

For the previous three years, Baylor basketball had been my identity. I had dedicated my time and effort to being the best player I could be so I could help my team be the best it could be. I tried to honor God with the way I lived because I believed my life had been blessed. Now, things were crumbling. I had been looking for any rays of hope since that team meeting, and I could see one here. Finally, we had some answers. Patrick had allegedly been killed by a former player, and no one else was suspected. That part of the story could end now. We would grieve for Patrick and his family, perhaps hold a memorial service, and then set out on the business of salvaging our season, my senior season.

The more optimistically I thought, the better I felt. Coach Bliss could not be held responsible for Dottie's actions because he had previously cut Dottie from the team. Harvey was coming in, and he was a six-eight player who supposedly possessed a guard's skill set. A player like him would make any team better. John, Lawrence, and Kenny weren't going anywhere. Our season didn't start until November, so we had more than three months to move on.

I needed time to get back to living the way I had before. I needed to stop partying, get right with God, get back into church, and start hanging with the right crowd again. I had a purpose once more.

This was a Monday—a great day for a fresh start. Hope renewed, I hopped off the couch and headed for school. Time to get back into my routine and work out.

On Day 2 of the comeback, a crack appeared in the facade. On Tuesday, July 22, Patrick Dennehy Sr. told a reporter that a Baylor coach helped to arrange payment for his son's education and living expenses. Mr. Dennehy said a Baylor coach had promised to "take care of" Patrick after he transferred to Baylor. He added that Patrick's girlfriend had talked to the NCAA about a car that a Baylor coach helped Patrick purchase.

Coach Bliss released a statement calling the story false. He was adamant that nothing illegal had happened. Coach's statements eased my fears over the report. Coach Bliss and Coach Ash had been coaching for thirty years. From my three years playing for them, I knew our coaches followed the rules. They wouldn't put themselves or our team at risk of NCAA sanctions. We didn't need to cheat to have a great team. I set aside any lingering doubts and headed for my workout.

On Thursday, another crack appeared. A new report stated that Patrick walked out of the basketball offices in the Ferrell Center with between $1,200 and $1,800 in cash and told his girlfriend a coach gave him the money to purchase a car. Coach Bliss and Patrick visited a dealership to check out a black 1996 Chevrolet Tahoe with a price tag of $10,000, including a $2,000 down payment. Patrick's father co-signed, and Patrick showed up a week later with cash for the down payment. To make matters worse, one media outlet reported that Patrick had told a former girlfriend he would receive a nice SUV for transferring to Baylor.

I finished reading the article and dropped my head, simultaneously sick and angry. *Cash for a car? Why would Coach Bliss go to a dealership with a player?*

News seemed to be breaking at a frenzied pace.

The next day, a badly decomposed body was discovered at a gravel pit not far from campus. In my heart, I knew it was Patrick.

Then word came that Baylor had appointed a three-man panel of law professors to investigate alleged violations within our program and hired a lawyer who was the former mayor of Austin to help them. This panel could prove to be the beginning of the end for our team. How could anything positive come from this investigation?

On Saturday, a media report said Dottie's wife alleged he received cash from Baylor coaches. She also said she had witnessed Dottie faking a drug test. According to her story, Dottie was given enough time to devise a means of cheating. She claimed numerous players failed the drug tests, including Patrick. Her story was detailed. She described how she drove Dottie and Patrick to a Waco clinic for their urine test. After the results came back positive, she was present when another player who was drug-free came to their apartment and gave Dottie a sample of his urine. She watched Dottie stuff the urine container into his pants while she drove Dottie and his teammates to a testing clinic.

I felt stupid. How could all this be going on without me knowing?

Dottie's wife wasn't through talking. She told the press that Dottie would have five or six teammates over to the apartment to smoke marijuana every day, including before practice. She said half of the group went to practice high.

Now, I was confused. I had rarely been drug tested in my three-plus years at Baylor. I had seen players taken out of practice to get tested, so I had to wonder how much of this story was true. I couldn't imagine any coach giving a player notice of a drug test nor allowing someone to re-test after a positive. Those would be major rules violations. Adding to my confusion was that I was learning of these alleged violations with what seemed to be the rest of America. How could I not know something?

Dottie's wife also claimed that when Dottie needed money about once a month, he went to the Ferrell Center and came out with $50 or $60. Then she said Dottie had been hearing voices in his head and having visions. Dottie had accused her of having an affair and began confronting teammates with his suspicions. She told Dottie's mother, who reportedly called the coaches and told them Dottie needed help. Baylor sent him to a therapist, but he stopped going. Dottie's wife left him when he accused her of cheating on him and made religious ramblings claiming he was a prophet. She wasn't describing the same Dottie I knew. Was I even a part of this team being talked about by the media?

I had barely finished pulling my jaw from the floor over the article when the TV touted more breaking news in the "Baylor men's basketball scandal." A medical examiner had identified the decomposed body as Patrick's. The truth hit: he was gone.

DEEPER INTO THE QUICKSAND

I ended the week I had decided to change my life by not going to church on Sunday. Church was a thing of the past now because I didn't want to feel bad for how I was living. I was trying to get by day to day. I wanted to have a moment of relief or normalcy from a summer straight from hell. In my mind, God had allowed all this to happen, so I would do my own thing from now on. I would take control of my happiness, my joy, and my peace. Besides, if all this mess would have occurred one year later, I would have been gone from Baylor, perhaps playing in a professional league somewhere. Instead, this was happening right before my senior year.

With every new media story, my team and my program slid deeper into the quicksand. It was a slow and painful death. The "me monster" kept growing more hostile.

When I was in the Ferrell Center to work out, the coaches hurried around with concerned expressions. I rarely spoke to any of them. We didn't need to talk. We were all caught in this quicksand, and we would soon go under.

On Monday, Coach Bliss came out firing through a lengthy news conference in which he asserted that Baylor did not buy cars for players and did not pay players. He said our basketball program was alive and well and was not out of control.

During this news conference, someone mentioned that attending Baylor cost more than $17,000 a year in tuition and fees. I had never thought about how much school cost—Baylor was paying at least $68,000 for my four years, not including housing, food, and books.

Once again, Coach Bliss handled the media's questions well. He spoke directly and clearly. He denied all allegations and said our program was clean. I wanted desperately to believe Coach, but it was beginning to become difficult to know what to believe.

Two days later, on Wednesday, *The Dallas Morning News* ran a story about Patrick's tuition. Reporter Jeff Miller had learned from Patrick Dennehy Sr. that Patrick was not on scholarship at Baylor. Patrick did not have a job, and his father had no idea how his son could afford to attend Baylor. Patrick's father also said he had not provided the $2,000 cash for the down payment on his son's Tahoe.

The possibility of a future NBA player not being on a full ride had never crossed my mind. How else could he be at Baylor at the cost of more than $17,000 a year? Patrick *had* to be on a scholarship because that was too much money for someone else to cover.

Once again, an unbelievable story had been topped by an even more unbelievable story. Each day produced new allegations and potentially new NCAA infractions. And the worst was yet to come.

9

DEATH OF A DREAM

My hands trembled as I held the newspaper. Gerry Fraley, a sports columnist with *The Dallas Morning News*, had written about us, and I read his column multiple times. In crystal-clear terms, Fraley contended that the only way to fix the problems at Baylor was to shut down the men's basketball program for one year and conduct an "exhaustive review" of our program.

I wanted to scream in protest! None of the allegations had been proved or even filed by the NCAA.

But the gravity of our situation hit me through Fraley's column. The allegations were so bad that someone was calling for a measure akin to the NCAA's so-called "death penalty." I realized that even if only a few charges stuck, we were in big trouble.

I sat aside the paper and decided to lift weights at the Ferrell Center. Perhaps I could tune everything out for a few hours there.

In the hallway leading to the locker room, I spotted assistant coach Abar Rouse walking toward me. This was Thursday, July 31—making it to the end of another month could feel like a milestone to celebrate—and Coach Rouse had reported for work on June 1. I'd had few interactions with him. As Coach Rouse and I neared each other, he looked worried. I had planned to walk past him, but something about his look convinced me he wanted to talk. I stopped.

"Crazy, everything going on, huh?" I asked.

He scanned the hallway in both directions before making eye contact with me.

"Ears everywhere," he said. "Gotta be careful."

I didn't know what to say, so I nodded.

Then as abruptly as he had stopped, he took off on his original path.

What was that all about? I wondered.

As I gathered my gear in the locker room, I rationalized that, like me, the coaches were freaking out. No telling what they were feeling or what they might say. I headed to the weight room, music turned up as loud as I could to drown out my thoughts.

My dad called the next day and told me he had been interviewed by a *Waco Tribune-Herald* reporter. In the article, several former players had come forward to say they had not seen any drug use in the program or any illegal payments. DeMarcus Minor talked at length about his *real* drug tests. His comments matched my experiences. Lawrence added his support for what DeMarcus said, as did Andrew White and Steve Raquet. I loved that our players had received an opportunity to fight back.

Dad was mentioned throughout the article. He detailed my experiences and observations, including two stories I had forgotten. Dad told the reporter he had to pay $15 for a media photo of me. He had tried to get it from the basketball office for my scrapbook but was required to purchase it. He also told of having to pay $1.50 for VHS tapes of games that weren't televised. He didn't believe the program could be so concerned about violating NCAA rules that it charged him $1.50 for each VHS tape while at the same time providing down payments for cars. Dad made an excellent point. It seemed like maybe some upset people were trying to stir up trouble. The article was fantastic because it revealed perspectives from within the program that had gone unreported.

I returned to the Ferrell Center that day to work out again. In the past, I had intentionally walked past the coaches' offices or made sure to bump into them on my way to shoot or lift. I wanted them to know I was putting in extra work to get better. But this time, I didn't want to see anyone. I took a back hall instead of my regular route and was shocked to see Coach Bliss suddenly appear.

I hadn't seen Coach for a few weeks, although it felt like months. Coach spotted me right after I saw him. I considering detouring down another hall to avoid him, but he was catching a lot of heat. The media were looking for dirt to dig up from his past, and I resented their tactics. Coach had taken me to speaking events. We had talked about basketball in his car. He had lifted me with his encouraging words in the elevator after I missed the free throws that knocked us out of the Big 12 tournament. After all Coach had done for me, I needed to repay him by encouraging *him*. I wanted Coach to know I had his back. That I was in this with him.

Coach looked beaten down. His face had lines I hadn't seen before. The positive, outgoing energy usually pouring out of him had been drained.

"Coach, I want you to know how sorry I am you are getting dragged through this. I just don't feel like you deserve this."

Coach lifted his head.

"Well, I really appreciate that, Matt," he said. "Let me talk to you for a minute."

"Yes, sir," I replied.

Coach led me down the hall to the coaches' locker room and closed the door behind me. It was just us two in the eerily quiet room.

Something was wrong with Coach. He wasn't making the direct eye contact he always made. I had watched him in countless speaking events. He recorded an instructional video about the Four Man Flex offense without making a mistake. Now, here he was, standing before me, his air of confidence missing.

"Matt, I need to tell you what's going on around here."

His hands motioned every direction even in that one sentence. He looked jittery.

"Patrick and Corey were not here on a scholarship."

He paused to gauge my reaction.

Patrick and Corey were actually walk-ons? Corey Herring had just completed his freshman season. In conversations with both, Patrick and Corey had given the impression they were on scholarship. I was confident they both *believed* they were on scholarship. With their talent, they could receive a scholarship from any school. *Had they turned down free rides elsewhere to walk on at Baylor?* Coach's admission was incredible.

"I went to Patrick's apartment. Matt, it was difficult to believe. I found a lot of money rolled up. And there were drugs. That's apparently how Patrick had been going to school. He was selling drugs to pay for school."

Coach seemed uneasy.

"Matt, I just wanted to tell you what happened. I wanted you to know."

My inner compass told me something wasn't right. But my coach-pleaser desperately wanted to believe him. I didn't want my mentor, the man who had taught me so much about basketball, to be a liar. Forced to choose between my inner compass and my coach-pleaser, the latter won.

"Yes, sir. I understand."

Coach's face softened, and his body relaxed.

"Great, Matt. I knew I could count on you to understand."

Coach Bliss patted me on the shoulder, and we left the room and headed our separate directions.

I talked with my dad later that day. I told him about the Waco paper's article and read his comments to him. Dad approved. He told me *The Dallas Morning News* had printed an article about a jailhouse interview with Dottie in which Dottie claimed he killed Patrick in self-defense after Patrick raised a weapon to shoot him. The world was back to bizarre. I was right back on that roller coaster ride. I decided not to tell my dad about the Coach Bliss meeting. At least not yet.

My encounter with Coach kept replaying in my mind. Something *was* really off. For the first time, I felt Coach had lied to me. I had been raised not to question anyone in authority. Should I start questioning my coach?

NO ALTERNATIVES

A week later, I still was thinking often about the conversation with Coach. More articles had come out, and the media scrutiny had intensified.

The most recent biggest blow had been an article in the *Fort Worth Star-Telegram* detailing newfound alleged NCAA violations at SMU while Coach Bliss was head coach there. The allegations included booster payments to star center Jon Koncak, who believed Coach Bliss was aware of the payments. Coach immediately fired back, saying in over thirty years of coaching in Division I, he had always followed NCAA rules.

I was walking to the SLC one day when reporters and cameras descended on me like vultures on roadkill.

"Do you know anything about payments to players?" one asked.

"How do you feel about what's going on?" another shouted at me.

As I ducked into the SLC, my phone went off. It was a *New York Times* reporter. I had escaped the media outside only to be reached by another reporter inside.

"Do you know anything about illegal drug use on your team?" he asked. "Did you receive any money to play at Baylor?"

No and no.

More reporters' calls came in while the media outside waited for me to reemerge. I felt trapped, as though the Baylor bubble was closing in on me.

Meanwhile, the university sent Coach Bliss, President Robert Sloan, Athletic Director Tom Stanton, and other VIPs to San Jose, California, for Patrick's burial—a sobering reminder of the personal tragedy at the center of the allegations and speculation.

Even while the university officials were in California, the stories kept flowing.

One detailed Coach Bliss's and assistant coach Rodney Belcher's presence at a pickup game involving Harvey Thomas before he signed with Baylor, the timing of which would violate NCAA rules. Another uncovered an issue Coach Bliss faced at New Mexico involving a player and a gun. That story described how a New Mexico player and his friend were in a car with a recruit while a gun was fired into the air. The player who fired the weapon was not charged with a crime, and Coach Bliss did not suspend the player, saying, "If every basketball player...that had a gun gave up his eligibility, we'd have fewer players." That quote sounded especially bad because now, at Baylor, that would be true.

Waco police announced that tests of the 9mm handgun found buried at the apartment complex revealed no link to Patrick's death. I didn't know if that was good news or bad news.

I had to get out of Waco, so I drove home to be with my parents. We tried to have conversations about ordinary topics, but we eventually found our way back to Baylor basketball. While I was home, my phone rang in my pocket. Because of all the media calls, I dreaded the phone ringing. I fielded as many media calls as I could handle, but I decided I needed a break. I reached for the phone to turn off the ringer and saw Coach Bliss's name on the display. I assumed he was still in California.

"Hey, Coach," I said.

"Matt, I need to talk to you about something important. Do you have time?"

He sounded tired and stressed, emotionless, almost robotic.

I mouthed, "Bliss" to my parents. They stopped their conversation.

I walked outside to the pool area and sat in a lounge chair.

"Yes, sir," I told him. "I have some time."

"Matt. I am going to be stepping down."

My mind immediately flashed back to my freshman year, right after I hit four three-pointers in our exhibition game, when Coach hugged me and said, "We are going to have four great years." I had believed him.

"I am going to announce it at a press conference," he continued, "and I would like you to be at the Ferrell Center. With everything that has happened—"

His voice trailed off. This was not the dynamic speaker I loved hearing. He sounded like he was reading a prepared statement.

Part of me wanted Coach to continue fighting. As far as I knew, no one had proved that he had lied or found him guilty of any violations. I wanted him to prove to everyone—and to me—that the allegations were untrue.

"Yes, sir," I said. "I understand. I'll be there."

"Thanks, Matt."

He ended the call.

I remained in the lounge chair in disbelief. My teammate Patrick was murdered at the hands of my former teammate Dottie. Our program was facing significant NCAA sanctions. And my mentor, a man I would run through a brick wall for, was leaving. It wasn't fair. I had done nothing wrong. I had worked hard and been a good person. And look what it brought me.

I walked inside with tears in my eyes and told my parents that Coach was leaving. They looked defeated. Mom and Dad had their dreams for me, and theirs were collapsing too. All the summer camps, the skills coaches, the select teams, the early morning drives, the evening pick-ups—all the sacrifices, wasted.

I walked past my parents and out the front door. It was evening, and it still was light outside. I walked into the grassy strip between the side-walk and the curb and watched the sun gradually disappear. Nothing bad had ever happened to me, and I couldn't understand why that was changing now. *Had I wasted all these years?*

After a half-hour of reflecting on the past, a switch inside of me flipped. I marched purposefully back inside the house.

"I need to figure out where I can go," I told my parents.

My dad said nothing. Mom looked sad and depressed. The "me monster" was taking control to keep my dream alive.

I pulled out my cell phone, filled with numbers I had accumulated over the past four years. I called a coach who had recruited me during high school. He was no longer at that school.

I looked up Logan's number next. But first, I thought back to that moment over a year ago when he told me he was leaving Baylor. I felt so stupid for wanting to persuade him to stay because he would miss out on something special there. Boy, had he made the right decision.

Logan answered right away and said he would call his coach, Bob McKillop, who called me within minutes and asked what he could do for me. I launched into my hurried sales speech. I was a hard worker. I wasn't a big scorer, but I was excellent at handling the ball and making good decisions. And he could ask Logan about me being a good teammate.

The coach stopped me.

"I'm very sorry for what you are going through," he said. "But we don't generally take one-year players."

Gut punch. But I wouldn't give up.

"I understand, Coach. Do you know of any other coach or program that might?"

"I'm sorry," he replied, "but I don't."

I did understand. It takes time to learn a system, and with one year of eligibility remaining, I didn't have that time. My only option was to go down with the ship. I filled in my parents and returned to the grassy strip out front. I retraced my journey from Berwick to The Colony, through all the pain and success at Baylor.

I had never envisioned this ending. I hadn't screwed up. I had done nothing illegal. I was paying for others' mistakes. I wondered where God was. *Where was He for Patrick and his family? Had I done something so terrible that I deserved to be caught in this mess?*

I didn't know that Mom was watching me through the large living room window, crying because her only son was suffering and she was helpless to ease his pain.

10

WHAT BAYLOR NEEDS

My phone rang again. It was a Waco number. I answered, and Heath Nielson, our director of media relations, was on the other end.

"How are you holding up?" he asked.

"Okay, I guess. What's up?"

I liked Heath, but I was beyond the point of manners and courtesy. I wanted to get straight to the purpose of his call.

"We are holding a meeting for the coaches, parents, and players on Monday," he told me. "No press allowed. Afterward, we are having a press conference, and President Sloan will make some remarks. We would like you to say a few words, answer questions from the media. I know you will do a good job."

As an incoming senior and one of the few players still on campus, I had been bombarded by reporters from all over the country, and I was sick of answering their questions. I did not want to speak to the media, and I didn't feel good about doing so. I only fielded their calls because I knew athletic department officials trusted me to respond to the tough questions as an unofficial team spokesman.

I considered turning down Heath's request. Then I did what I always did.

"Yes, sir. I'll be there."

"Great, Matt. See you there. Thanks!"

Of course, by the time Monday arrived, a whole news cycle's worth of events had already taken place.

On Friday, Baylor announced the resignations of Coach Bliss and Athletic Director Tom Stanton. I later learned that school officials had confronted Coach about the allegations of payments to Patrick and Corey. Coach supposedly confessed to paying for some or all of their tuition. Then Coach was asked about reports that he had attended a pickup game involving Harvey Thomas and the alleged violations of Baylor's drug-testing policy.

I guess the allegations were too much to fight because Coach submitted his resignation.

The alleged violations were significant. I knew the NCAA would bring the hammer down if they were true, and I was one of the nails that would be struck.

The announcement also contained unexpected news that President Sloan had decided to get out in front of potential NCAA punishment and impose immediate sanctions on our program. He announced a new drug-testing policy and placed our program on at least two years' probation. He also canceled any postseason appearances for the 2003–04 season—including the Big 12 tournament. Because of the postseason ban, my dream was dead. Because of others' actions, I had no chance of playing in the NCAA Tournament. The Big Dance was the carrot coaches dangled in front of us. We did the running, lifting, film watching, and traveling all for a chance to win enough games to be selected to play on our sport's biggest stage.

President Sloan explained that current players would receive an unconditional release to transfer to another school if they wished. That was a generous offer on his part, but it did nothing for me. As a senior, I was stuck at Baylor. I certainly couldn't blame any teammate who wanted to bolt for a team eligible for the postseason.

I drove back to Waco on Sunday, and the two-and-a-half hours alone in the car provided plenty of time to think, especially about Patrick's funeral. I had not lost anyone close to me before Patrick. I cringed at the thought of how excruciating it would be for my parents to bury me. I could not fathom what Patrick's parents and family thought as they said goodbye to their son. They had to have been thrilled when they found out he would be attending Baylor, and they probably felt secure knowing that he would be safe and taken care of by his coaches. Instead, only his ashes returned home.

Reading the words spoken about Patrick at his funeral reminded me of the countless times he had goofed around with us. He had a good heart and was a kind person, and with his unique character, we never knew what we would get from him. He possessed immense basketball potential, and I could only wonder how far he would have gone as a player.

As I drove, I tried to envision what our team would look like. I still had too many questions to get a clear picture, but I knew it would not be pretty.

A new coach would be coming in. Who could they possibly persuade to take over our program? What coach in his right mind would willingly accept our position? What about our incoming freshmen and transfers who had committed to being here? Would they decide to go elsewhere? Then there were our returning players. Would they accept President

Sloan's offer and transfer? A number of schools would covet taking our top players from us. Was there any possible way to keep them?

That night, my nervousness about the news conference kept me from sleeping well. I couldn't remember the last night I had slept peacefully anyway. Everything to that point had seemed so unreal, like it was happening to someone else. But the next day would make it real. Coach Bliss would meet with us, and then he would be gone for good. Our team would be together, but we would be missing Patrick. I also tried to anticipate what questions the media would ask me. Would I be able to keep my composure and do the job the university had assigned to me?

I was twenty-one years old, but I was a naïve twenty-one. I had led a pretty charmed life—my parents were still together, we hadn't suffered any unexpected deaths or tragedies in my family, and I had been successful in almost everything I attempted. Now I was facing some very adult issues that I hadn't seen coming. The pressure seemed unfair. The weight of the Baylor basketball program, or what remained of it, seemed to sit on top of me. The more I thought about the next morning, the more frightened I became.

I felt utterly alone as I dreaded what sunlight would bring. Anger and rage filled my heart. *Why did all this happen? Should I pray? Would that do any good?* I stared at the ceiling until my eyes could stay open no longer.

NOT THE PROMISED ENDING

What is the dress code for a news conference announcing that a program is being dismantled? I selected a long-sleeved, white cotton shirt with a pair of well-worn faded blue jeans. Then, I put on my favorite sandals. I checked my look in the mirror and rolled up my sleeves and untucked my shirt. I wanted to portray a casual, comfortable, loose style. With a deep breath, I walked out the door.

I pulled into the Ferrell Center parking lot and left Blink-182 playing for a few minutes. I wanted to delay the inevitable.

Right or wrong, my entire life was wrapped up in basketball. As long as basketball was good, then my relationship with God was good. Now that basketball was in disarray, my relationship with God was nonexistent. I had never thought about needing an exit strategy from basketball. I had never thought of life without the sport. Since fourth grade, I had worked and focused on basketball. It had become the idol of my life. But now, my life was changing all around me.

The team meeting was in the media room, the location of postgame media conferences. When I walked in, most of my teammates were present. I hadn't seen many of them for most of the summer, and I understood why they stayed out of Waco. Many of the players' family members were in attendance, and there was not the typical mingling and catching up. Coach Bliss sat off by himself. I recognized a few other Baylor officials, including President Sloan. I took a seat next to my dad, who drove down that morning to be with me.

After the chairs filled, Coach Bliss stood at the front of the room and told us he had resigned because he was responsible for the mess we were in. He said he wanted the very best for us and encouraged us to stay with the program, wishing us the best season possible. His speech came across as rehearsed and business-like, and it ended about as abruptly as it had started.

I watched as Coach returned to his seat. This was not the ending he had painted for my mom and me on our recruiting visit.

I was asked to say a few words to our team. The request caught me off-guard because I had been thinking about what I would say at the news conference to come, not here. When I stood, I suddenly knew why I was so terrified to get up and speak. At this moment, Baylor needed me to be a leader, a person who would be pro-Baylor and say all the right things. Baylor needed me to be who I had been for the past three years. But I no longer was that person. To speak with excitement and optimism about Baylor basketball now, I would have to lie. *Should I be honest and let people know how much of a no-win situation we were stuck in? Or should I try to spin some story filled with hope and positivity?* I made my decision and gripped the podium.

"I truly believe that what happened over the summer was an isolated event," I said. "I think we can still have an awesome season. We get to go to Hawaii, and that's pretty cool. We still get to play Texas and Kansas and all the Big 12 teams. I welcome and encourage all of you to stay because I am staying. Let's show the rest of the country what we are all made of."

I had intended to project strength through loyalty, but the truth was that I had not *decided* to stay. I was here only because I had nowhere else to go. And our season would be pointless. If our best players left, the only thing that would be *awesome* would be the margins by which our opponents beat us. There would be no postseason. No Big 12 Tournament. There was no prize at the end of the race. The only thing I would be playing for was my tuition and meals, which would allow me to receive the speech communications degree I had chosen because I had no idea what else to do and the seniors before me had said it was the easiest to complete.

Since my youth, I had played to win the prize. Paul's words in 1 Corinthians 9:24 had been burned into my thoughts: *"Do you not know that in a race all the runners run, but only one gets the prize? Run in such a way as to get the prize."* But how could I convince the others to stay if we knew before starting the race that we couldn't win? Sure, there were important traits like pride, integrity, and loyalty. But they had always been wrapped around the brick of winning glory.

I left the podium thinking, *What a poor con job.*

A few others spoke, but I tuned them out. My job for the day wasn't over, and questions were coming my way.

MEET THE PRESS

I was escorted upstairs to a makeshift media room on the arena concourse. The news conference was already underway, and reporters and cameras were scattered everywhere. A green curtain with gold "BU" logos hung loosely behind a podium draped with a small banner reading "Baylor University."

I watched President Sloan answer questions at the conclusion of his speech. He was a pro at handling the speed and variety of the media's questions. I had some experience with media interviews, but nothing had prepared me for this.

When my name was announced, cameras turned to record my walk to the podium. En route, I realized I was grossly underdressed. President Sloan and Heath both wore a coat and tie. Other prominent officials had dressed like bankers. Then here I came, strolling up in sandals and blue jeans with my shirt untucked and sleeves rolled up. Casual, comfortable, and loose didn't seem appropriate in this setting.

Heath had coached me on potential questions. He laid out a broad theme for me of being pro-Baylor and staying positive. He told me to relax, which he understood was easier said than done. In normal times, I would have had no problem relaxing. I had always felt like an ambassador not only for the men's basketball program but for the university as well. But as I adjusted the microphone, I knew I had to fake it. I was about to tell some lies.

"Matt, are you returning to play for Baylor next year?"

Stay positive. Don't let them see any doubt.

"Yes, I have decided I am going to stay. Along with that, I talked to R.T., who is staying, and Terrance Thomas."

There was no decision to stay. I wanted to leave and couldn't. Neither could R.T. because he also was a senior. Although I appreciated R.T. and Terrance staying, we were stuck in this no-win situation.

"Why are you coming back?"

Tough question.

"I can't speak for them, but for me, it's because I love the university. I came here half for Coach Bliss, half because I knew what Baylor stands for, the Christian background that it has. I love the campus, love the students, have many friends here, and of course the Baylor degree—it's a good thing to have."

Actually, my friends had changed how they approached me and how they spoke to me. And with my new party habits, not many of them were interested in receiving my drunk phone calls at 2 a.m., sobbing about how things used to be. Around Waco and on campus, the students looked at me like I carried a contagious disease. I had dropped my Christian practices. And my degree was an afterthought.

"Have you ever been offered money or know of any such payments?"

Apparently, I wasn't that good! My family paid $1.50 for VHS tapes.

"I've never been aware of anything."

"Do you know anything about the allegations of drug use on the team?"

Are you asking whether, while watching a movie with my friends or attending church or FCA events with Coach Bliss, I had seen anyone light up a joint or fake a drug test? I hadn't, which made me feel stupid for being so naïve.

"In my three years, I've never once noticed anything or saw anything or heard anything, so I don't know what that's all about."

"What are you looking for in a new coach?"

I liked what I had with Coach Bliss. He was what I wanted and what I was supposed to have my senior year.

"Dr. Sloan depicted the kind of coach that we'd like to have. And we had a great one. Coach Bliss was one of the greatest men I've ever known. He taught me a lot about life and basketball. I really believe someone in his line would be a good coach."

The questions increased in intensity. I tried to calmly answer each one with the same matter-of-fact voice. As we reached the end, one reporter asked the million-dollar question.

"With all that has happened, how can you go out and play and have a normal season?"

Let's see if I have this straight. One teammate was murdered, shot in the head by a former teammate. Another player was also suspected at one point. There are witnesses who saw players use drugs and fake drug tests. We are going to get hammered by the NCAA on top of the penalties already self-imposed. Our top players may leave, and we don't have a head coach. Did I miss anything?

"It's just to be able to compete because no matter what, postseason or not, we're going to be able to play against good players in the Big 12. And we're going to Hawaii, you know. Who doesn't want to do that? It's just the honor in it, too. We have nothing to lose. We're going to play hard and try to gain people's respect as we go, and maybe get a couple of wins along the way."

I survived the questions. I had told the lies I needed to tell to hopefully keep things together. Heath and President Sloan shook my hand as I walked down the stairs and thanked me for my commitment to Baylor. My dad was waiting for me at the bottom. We talked for a few minutes before he hugged me and left for Dallas.

Walking out to my car, I felt dazed. I didn't know where to go. Home? A bar?

I wanted to feel nothing.

EVEN WORSE?

As the search for Coach Bliss's replacement commenced, the media speculated about John Lucas II—John's father—as a potential head coach. That idea intrigued me. If John's dad became our coach, John would stay. If John stayed, perhaps Lawrence and Kenny would too. They were 60 percent of our total offense the past season, and their staying was the path to us at least being competitive. A few other names were thrown out for discussion, but I wondered who would be dumb enough or desperate enough to take this job. With the first game less than three months away, the talent pool had to be pretty shallow.

The media questions kept coming at me, and I needed to get away. I decided to visit my former coach, Steve Yoder, in Pennsylvania.

In all the time I had spent with Coach Steve, drinking was never one of our activities. As we sat around partaking and playing cards, it felt good not to be around Baylor basketball. At one point, Coach Steve brought up his opinion of me remaining at Baylor. "There is something to be said about loyalty," he said. Although he was proud of me, I didn't see any opportunities I had in staying. And the idea of loyalty didn't mean much to me anymore.

We were kicking back in his living room late one night when my cell phone rang. That familiar sick feeling in my stomach that had accompanied phone calls returned. I pulled my phone out of my pants pocket. It was almost 11 p.m. At that hour, a call from Heath couldn't be good.

"What's up, Heath?"

"Hey, Matt. You need to be ready for tomorrow. It's about to get worse."

I couldn't imagine the situation possibly getting worse.

"Just make sure you check the papers tomorrow," he said. "And have your phone on you at all times."

Even in Pennsylvania, I couldn't escape the roller-coaster ride.

I tossed and turned throughout the night in the Yoders' guest room. I had hoped Coach Steve would let me sleep in late. His knock on the bedroom door early in the morning ended that hope.

"You should get up," he told me.

I grumbled a response and dragged my way downstairs. Coach was sitting at the kitchen table reading a newspaper with a steaming cup of coffee in his hand. As I approached, he slid the paper around to face me.

A wire story reported that the *Fort Worth Star-Telegram* had interviewed Abar Rouse, the new assistant coach who had warned me about "ears everywhere." Coach Rouse had secretly recorded multiple conversations involving Coach Bliss a little more than two weeks earlier.

"What we've got to create here is drugs," Coach Bliss had been recorded saying as he revealed a plan to portray Patrick as a drug dealer to explain how he was able to attend Baylor.

Other quotes attributed to Bliss in the article were astonishing:

- "Our whole thing right now, we can get out of it, okay? Reasonable doubt is there's nobody right now that can say we paid Patrick Dennehy." After Rouse said he understood, Bliss added, "Because he's dead."

- "…Dennehy is never going to refute what we say. I've got some things to say about him, because he came in and tried to get me to help him with something, and I told him, 'I can't help you.' Now I know that ticked him off, but he knows that's the truth. And now he's dead, so he isn't going to argue with me at all."

- In a conversation with an unidentified player: "First of all, nobody is ever going to know about the fact you might have smoked weed with the guys. I think the thing we want to do— and you think about this—if there's any way that we can create the perception that Pat may have been a dealer…even if we had to kind of make some things look a little better than they are, that can save us. And the part about it is, we don't deserve to be in a jam, so I don't mind. And I'm not telling you to lie at all, although, you know, I'm already lying a little bit to the people because there are some things I don't know because Pat's dead."

◆   In a conversation with a player and Rouse: "The reason we're in this jam is because of a dead guy and the guy that murdered him, and that isn't fair for you and me and Abar to be in this jam, because we didn't do anything. It's not like we created this situation. We're the victims. If you read the papers, [expletive], I'm the bad guy."

I had no question that those were Coach Bliss's words. He had a particular way of saying things that came through in the quotes.

The quotes were, in essence, the same story Coach had told me the day we bumped into each other at the Ferrell Center—the story he needed others to believe. And he had presented it so matter-of-fact to me because he knew I would believe him. I had wondered that day if Coach had lied to me. Reading this article removed any doubt. The man I had placed my trust in had lied to me.

I had witnessed plenty of bizarre antics from Coach, but they had all been in the context of basketball, when I believed he was trying to get us to care more and play harder. But this type of desperation and deceit was difficult to process. He had not even stopped short of trying to pin the blame on a dead guy—a young man he had recruited to play for him.

To think of all the times I had defended Coach after the reports started coming out...

The last statement of Bliss I read that morning said, "And we are gonna win. I'll tell you, like, I just spent two hours with our lawyer. He's a [expletive]. That's why he told me, 'Just give me reasonable doubt.' He said, 'This is the first time they've ever had an NCAA investigation with a dead person.' So we don't have to have overwhelming evidence. All we've got to have is any reasonable doubt, because I've got thirty years in the business with no bad track record."

I put the newspaper aside and headed for the shower. I needed to wash off all the stink.

As I showered, I thought of our next head coach. There was no way the university would find anyone with any kind of a future to take this job. It already was August 16; all the good, clean coaches had jobs. No one was going to move down to a job at Baylor. The university could probably find an assistant at a top program who had never been a head coach. But who would want to step into this mess for their first head coaching job? SMU's football program had received the NCAA's death penalty in 1987. That was sixteen years earlier, and SMU football still had not fully recovered. Who would sign up for basketball's version of that mess?

LET THE EXITS BEGIN

When I returned to Waco, I learned that Lawrence was transferring to Mississippi State. I didn't get to say goodbye, although I understood him leaving so quickly. I knew his departure was just the beginning. With our best player leaving for a better situation, the rest would follow. I was jealous and angry that I could not do the same.

Kenny, who led the Big 12 in three-pointers made, was the next to leave, transferring to the University of Texas. At least Lawrence left for a different conference. *How could Kenny go to another Big 12 school? And to add insult to injury, he had to choose Texas?*

Would we even have a team? That thought hadn't crossed my mind until now. *But what if we didn't have enough players to play?*

Late in the afternoon on Thursday, August 21, I was putting on a fresh shirt to go out and find a distraction. Less than a year ago, I had never tasted a drop of alcohol. Now it was my only release. Most of the students hadn't returned from summer break, so the bars weren't crowded. That meant fewer people to recognize me.

A close friend called and asked if I had heard the news. I cringed. I had heard that phrase too many times lately.

"No," I answered. "What now?"

"They have hired a new head coach."

"Who is it?" I asked.

"His name is Scott Drew," my friend said. "He is coming from Valparaiso. Have you heard of him?"

"Nope. Never heard of him."

Growing up in Berwick, Pennsylvania, Matt Sayman dedicated himself to improving his basketball game. His coaches loved him because he was eager to figure out what they wanted and why.

Matt convinced his family to move to Texas so he could attend The Colony High School.

Sayman anchors BU ship

Junior guard steadies young Bears, playing 'coach's best friend' role

By JOHN WERNER
Tribune-Herald staff writer

Matt Sayman is usually a footnote instead of a headline.

You'll never see him throw down a spectacular dunk or woo the crowd with an Iversonesque crossover dribble. In 85 career games, Sayman has led Baylor in scoring once.

Basketball is much more than flash and dash. Sayman is a steadying influence who can keep a team from falling apart at critical moments. His head is in the right place, and that's something often overlooked by fans and media.

"Matt is a coach's best friend," said Baylor coach Dave Bliss. "He does a terrific job of keeping things together. He knows what he should be doing at all times, and he has a great attitude regardless of what role you give him."

Since Sayman stepped into the starting lineup, the Bears have won three of their last five games. Sayman collected 18 assists and 11 rebounds during Baylor's three-game winning streak over Oklahoma State, Kansas State and Nebraska.

Scoring isn't important to Sayman. He feels he's done his job if he gets the ball inside to Lawrence Roberts or R.T. Guinn or sets up guards John Lucas or Kenny Taylor on the perimeter.

"They don't need me to take shots away from the other guys," Sayman said. "I was never a big scorer in high school (at

> "Sometimes, I walk out on the court and can't believe I'm playing against these guys. They're all big, tough and strong. You're not going to catch a break against anybody in the Big 12."
>
> BU's Matt Sayman

An article in the *Waco Tribune-Herald* during Matt's junior year touted his "steadying influence" on the team.

From left, Matt, R.T. Guinn, Will Allen, Tommy Swanson and Turner Phipps listen during Coach Scott Drew's first press conference in the Ferrell Center.

Matt fields questions from the media during Coach Drew's first press conference.

Matt stands beside Coach Drew as the players, coaches, and fans sing "That Good Old Baylor Line" during Midnight Madness.

The Baylor Bears and coaches observe a moment of silence for Patrick Dennehy prior to their regular-season opener against Texas Southern.

R.T. Guinn, Matt Sayman, and Terrance Thomas remained at Baylor for their senior year.

Matt played thirty-seven minutes during the leftovers' game against Texas Southern University—spending just three minutes of game time off the court.

A billboard advertises Baylor basketball, including the women's team at right. Shown at left are Terrance Thomas sprinting down the court, R.T. Guinn releasing a shot, and Matt directing his teammates.

Matt (13), Coach Scott Drew, Carl Marshall (10), and R.T. Guinn (34)
huddle up during a game.

The Baylor Bears and coaches pose for an official team photo during
Matt's senior year.

The Baylor Bears huddle before a game in the Ferrell Center.

Watching a game, from left, are coaches Jerome Tang, Matthew Driscoll, Scott Drew, Mark Morefield, and Paul Mills.

A poster thanked the Baylor senior players for sticking with the program.

Corey Herring (5), Matt Sayman (13), Harvey Thomas (15), and the other Bears charge forward as the team comes back in the second half against Kansas State for their final home game.

Matt raises his fist to the crowd during Senior Night after the Bears'
final home game of the 2003–2004 season.

R.T. Guinn, Matt Sayman, and Terrance Thomas play the Oklahoma Sooners
during their final game as Baylor Bears.

Matt broke the Baylor career record for games played (118).

Matt, second from left, kept his lucky number 13 to play professional basketball in Iceland, helping Njardvik win the championship in 2005

Coach Scott Drew says Matt and the other "leftovers" played an integral role in helping the Baylor Bears win the 2021 NCAA men's basketball championship.

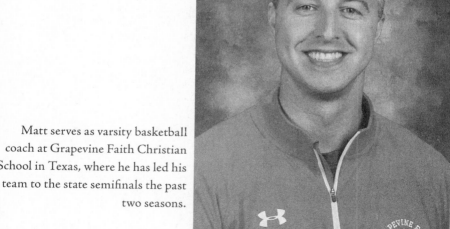

Matt serves as varsity basketball coach at Grapevine Faith Christian School in Texas, where he has led his team to the state semifinals the past two seasons.

11

HOPE IN THE FUTURE?

On Tuesday, August 26, I had an appointment I could not have anticipated when I stepped onto campus three years earlier. Our new head coach would be meeting with the leftover players—in the baseball locker room, of all places. In order to avoid any unwanted publicity, the meeting was set for the baseball stadium across the large parking lot from the Ferrell Center, where the media would expect us to gather.

I couldn't blame the athletic department for trying to hide us. I had been hiding plenty myself. I had always loved the energy on campus as students returned from the summer. This year, my stomach was in knots. The nation had been following the events surrounding Patrick's murder and the ensuing scandal. Our student body would have closely followed the news.

I dreaded the looks and questions I was sure to field, even from students I had never met but who would recognize my face or name. *Would they come back to campus angry or resent the players who stayed? Would they throw us into the same boat as those who had actually done wrong?* Fortunately, as the campus refilled for the fall semester, I went largely unrecognized because I kept my head firmly pointed down as I walked across campus, a cap shading my eyes.

Based on how my parents raised me, I knew I needed to give the new coaching staff the benefit of the doubt and trust they were here to help us win games and would sincerely care about us. But the summer's events jaded the way I approached their arrival.

In my mind, there was no way they truly wanted this job. Surely, they had accepted only because they saw an opportunity in the situation. But that opportunity ultimately would come down the road at another school after they had weathered this storm. There was no way they believed we could win. I figured they were handed a free pass in the Big 12 with no expectations for specific victory totals this season and, possibly, for the next few years.

Before I met my new coaches, I already did not trust them because I had trusted Coach Bliss, and he had lied to me.

I had never been a leftover. None of my coaches had taught me how to be one. But we had all been relegated to leftover status. I felt like I was on the Island of Misfit Toys from that Rudolph the Red-Nosed Reindeer Christmas movie.

What would these new coaches want with the leftovers?

Four days earlier, I had attended the media conference at the Ferrell Center introducing Coach Drew as our new coach. The athletics staff set aside several rows of seats for the players. When I arrived, only a few players were there: R.T., Terrance, Tommy Swanson, Will Allen, and incoming freshman Turner Phipps. Our first game was less than three months away, and I wondered who else we could find to fill our roster.

Every program went through turnover each year. Players graduated, left early for the NBA, incurred injuries, or gave up the sport for various reasons. New players were recruited to replace them. That's the way college basketball worked. In a typical year, we replaced about six players. Two or three would be seniors, so their departure could be anticipated. The rest were usually guys who had not received much playing time the season before. Rarely must a team unexpectedly replace its key contributors.

Our 2002–03 team had two seniors. Nobody was leaving early for the NBA. We should have had twelve players returning plus two incoming freshmen and Patrick becoming eligible.

Instead, we lost ten players.

Three took advantage of the special waiver offer and transferred without losing a season's worth of eligibility: John to Oklahoma State, Lawrence to Mississippi State, and Kenny to Texas. The NCAA granted incoming freshman Tyrone Nelson, a six-ten center, a release from the letter-of-intent he had signed to play at Baylor. He found a spot at Grambling State. (He played there one year and transferred to New Mexico State, where he started for two seasons.) Steve Raquet, the hard-working walk-on, and incoming transfer Robert Hart had left the school.

Then, of course, we'd lost Patrick, and Dottie was gone.

Ten players lost in one summer because of graduation, transfer, tragedy, and termination.

I preferred thinking of how our locker room was supposed to look.

I grew up reading Bible stories like David and Goliath from 1 Samuel 17:32–51. I understood about winning in impossible situations as David did. Trusting in God's power over any situation enabled men of God to accomplish remarkable feats. But this felt more like David walking into battle carrying a fly swatter instead of a slingshot.

As the NCAA continued to look into the allegations against our program, we had a few players who had not been cleared to play. Who knew what would happen with them? They could be arrested, get cut from the team, be slapped with a suspension, or transfer to another school. Anything was possible.

I thought about how taxing and physically draining it was to play against the Texas Longhorns' deep roster. How they would throw wave after wave of players at us. How could we survive? Even with our studs last year, Oklahoma State's defensive pressure had forced us into running our offense up around half-court. Would we even be able to cross half-court now?

This was going to be a brutal season.

I decided to park by the Ferrell Center and walk across the parking lot to the baseball complex. Out of the corner of my eye, I noticed a bronze car that I immediately recognized as belonging to Coach Brian O'Neill, one of our former assistants. He had invested hours in me, working on my footwork and shot, so I went over to say hello.

He didn't say much to me about what had happened over the summer, and to be honest, I didn't want to know what he knew and didn't know. The last thing he told me was, "I met with your new coach, and he is really good." Saying goodbye to Coach O'Neill was difficult because that was the last interaction I would have with the staff that brought me to Baylor.

ENERGETIC, OPTIMISTIC—AND YOUNG!

The baseball locker room was a strange place for a basketball team to meet. But why not? Strange had become the new normal.

I took a seat and caught a glimpse of the future of Baylor basketball. Seeing my fellow senior R.T. was a welcomed sight because I knew I could rely on him. Terrance was our other senior. I was surprised he stayed. But then again, throughout his interesting junior season, I had been surprised numerous times that he hadn't left or been told to leave. Terrance hugged me as soon as he saw me. He couldn't have been happy about our situation either, but he had a believable smile on his face. Although I was thankful R.T. and Terrance were there, we needed more.

Only a few seats in the locker room were occupied. I spotted our lone incoming scholarship freshman, Carl Marshall, a five-eleven guard from Chicago. For some reason, Carl had chosen to honor his commitment to enroll despite the NCAA out he could have taken. Perhaps he saw the potential for a ton of playing time as a freshman. I knew almost nothing about his high school career or his ability.

Turner was our only other incoming freshman at that time, a walk-on listed at six-one. That was a stretch. He was from Lubbock—the home of Texas Tech—and he gave great effort but lacked experience at this level. Coach Bliss had allowed him to join as a walk-on at the beginning of the summer. Turner had believed he could earn playing time, even after Bliss told him in a casual pickup game, "Stop shooting—that's not your job." I shook my head, knowing that Turner didn't understand yet how it worked here. Now, though, he might have a shot at playing.

Ryan Pryor also had come early on during the summer as a walk-on transfer from a junior college. Ryan was one of the few teammates I spent much time with outside of basketball. I had already grown to appreciate Ryan's friendship as we processed each revelation that was sprung on us.

Will was another walk-on who could expect to see playing time, and it certainly would help us to have another player transitioning with us to this new regime. Will had been a very good high school player and could really shoot. But similar to most walk-ons, he was a step slower than most scholarship players. As a freshman the previous season, he had played a total of three minutes spread over three games. At the end of some practices, he would be walking off the floor, and one of us would ask if he had gotten in that day. He would jokingly compare himself to Michael Jordan and say that he was saving his knees.

I liked all these guys, but I wasn't sure how much they could help us on the floor.

A door opened, and in walked Matthew Driscoll, one of the new assistant coaches. At thirty-nine, he was the oldest on the coaching staff. He had been an assistant at Wyoming and Clemson, and he had worked with Coach Drew for all of seven weeks before coming to Baylor with him. What Coach Driscoll lacked in size, he more than made up for with energy that seemed to be dripping from him as he moved toward the front of the room at almost a jog's pace.

Coach Driscoll talked for a few minutes. He knew our names, our positions, and other details about us. Granted, we didn't have a full roster of players to learn yet, but he impressed me with his effort. He focused on how things were looking up for Baylor basketball.

Looking up? Look around! There is nothing "up" about this situation.

Coach Driscoll then introduced the main act, and through the door came a very young-looking man. At thirty-two, Coach Drew was one of the youngest among the more than 300 head coaches in Division I.

He came to us from Valparaiso University, or Valpo as it's often nicknamed. It's located in Valparaiso, Indiana, a city of 30,000. All I knew about Valpo dated back to my high school years, when I watched Bryce Drew nail an ESPY-award-winning buzzer-beater for Valpo in the NCAA Tournament. It turned out that Bryce was Coach Drew's younger brother. Their father was Homer Drew, who as head coach turned Valpo into a prominent mid-major program. Coach Drew had been part of that process as one of his father's assistant coaches before taking over the program when his father retired.

But Valparaiso was not Baylor.

Coach Drew had been a head coach for one full year. The previous season, he led Valparaiso to a 20–11 record, the Mid-Continent Conference regular-season championship, and an appearance in the NIT. But now he was stepping into arguably the strongest conference and would coach not only against the league's future NBA players but also its Hall of Fame-level head coaches.

Coach Bliss had been a D-I head coach for twenty-eight years, and Doug Ash had been his assistant at every stop along the way. Coaches Bliss and Ash had been coaching together for almost as long as Coach Drew had been alive. With Coach Bliss's experience and gift for scouting opponents, he had us prepared each game. He didn't buckle in big situations. He was cool and calm when we needed him to be because whatever the circumstances, he had been there before.

I questioned whether Coach Drew could bring the same presence—not from lack of ability but lack of experience. Then I almost laughed out loud at the thought that it wouldn't matter this season! This coach would need to know how to dress nicely and say the appropriate words to the media after each fifty-point loss.

Coach Drew entered the room with an optimistic walk. He looked like he wanted us to see that he was joining a program consisting solely of winners. He wore a new Baylor polo shirt. He had the same dark hairstyle he has today (although he had slightly more hair back then) and an excited, "I'm ready for this" smile. But, boy, did he look young.

Coach introduced his assistant coaches. They also looked young. They *were* young.

Then he started telling us how sorry he was for everything we had gone through. I heard only parts of his speech because I struggled to stay engaged. Thinking about how far our program and I had fallen to reach this moment drowned out the words I'm sure he had carefully crafted for his new players. We weren't supposed to be in this situation. I would rather be hearing Coach Bliss's "I'm not your friend" speech with John and Lawrence sitting beside me.

I do remember Coach Drew saying something about attitude, and I heard the word *hope* a few times. One phrase that stuck with me was that we were supposed to "hope and look forward to the future."

I couldn't imagine how he expected us to believe in hope and the future. Especially those of us who knew better. Just six months earlier, we had lost a game at Oklahoma by forty-nine points, and that was with a full roster of scholarship players!

What hope? What future with this group?

"It's time to look past the summer and to focus on basketball," he said. But in my mind, the events of the summer surrounded us in a never-lifting fog.

One of the last things he told us was, "You're the start of something special. Future teams will have success because of what you are going to do."

He said this as though he believed it. His assistant coaches looked like they probably believed it. But I didn't think any of us players did.

RAISED EXPECTATIONS

By the time we stood to leave the locker room, I couldn't wait to get out of there.

Coach Driscoll tapped my shoulder and motioned for me to stay behind.

"Coach Drew wants to visit with you," he said.

Me? What could I have done already?

I walked back toward the indoor batting cages. Coach Drew was already seated, an empty chair for me in front of him.

"Matt," he told me, "I have heard really good things about you. You have meant a lot to this program. The players look up to you, and I am really going to lean heavily on you this year."

My teammates had looked up to me, and I had led behind the scenes in the past. It was a role I cherished. But this was not my team!

"I know this is not how you envisioned your senior year to be, but there can be a lot of good that comes out of this. We can only control what we do now. With that said, I need you to do more."

I had never in three years been asked to do more. I had done what was expected and then went above and beyond that. I was the one my coaches measured others' efforts against. I showed up to practice, gave maximum effort, loved my role, and was never questioned.

I nodded.

"Matt, I need to get each of these guys fully on board with what we are doing here."

What are we doing here exactly? Surviving? Just getting by?

"I want you to take each player out to lunch individually. Make sure they are buying into the team. Convince them that there is hope in looking to the future. Can you do that?"

Do I have a choice? I didn't spend too much time with basketball players outside of the Ferrell Center. And to be honest, that decision had kept me out of investigations surrounding the summer's events.

I answered, "Yes, sir."

"I also need you to be the media guy. I need you to be the go-to guy for Heath and always be ready to speak to the press if need be. Can I count on you for that?"

Can I say no? I haven't been allowed to refuse anything yet!

"Yes, sir. I understand."

"Finally," Coach continued, "I need you to be in the best shape of your life. You will be playing more minutes than you ever have before. I need you to burn another 500 calories each day on top of what we are doing as a team. Terrance is doing the same thing. Do you understand what I am asking?"

Asking? You are telling me, just in a polite way. Like a father to a son. No, like an older brother.

I was too defensive to take any of our conversation the proper way. I didn't appreciate his questioning my conditioning and work ethic. After a coach gave me my workout sheet, I hit it hard. There was no need to tell me to do more.

In reality, everything Coach Drew was saying was spot on. I didn't see it at the time, and I would be lying if I said it wasn't until much later in life when I realized why he asked me to do those things. It *had* to come from me. I was heavier than ever, mainly because of the partying that had become almost an every night thing, including eating anything in sight. If Coach Bliss had given me these instructions, I would have followed them blindly. But my anger and resentment blinded me now.

"Yes," I said.

Just let me get out of here, please.

"Thanks, Matt. I know there is great opportunity for you this season."

His upbeat attitude annoyed me.

"Yes, sir."

Coach Bliss had rarely asked for our opinions. When he did, it was evident he wanted our answers to be in line with what he had already said. I excelled at that.

I couldn't tell Coach Drew that I was not bought in. I had been a coach's dream player in junior high, high school, and my first three seasons at Baylor. But I had been betrayed. My wound was deep and still open. I couldn't tell my head coach how I felt. That the whole situation sucked. That I didn't like being on campus with students asking me questions because they wanted more information. That I wanted things to be the way they had been when the summer started. That, nothing against him, I was mad he even was *my coach*. That we weren't going to be any good.

This was the exact opposite of my dream.

When I look back to that point, I can see my faith had been stripped down to where I realized what I had believed for so long was wrong. I had fallen into the trap of a false theology that said as long as I acted like a Christian, God would bless my life by allowing me to accomplish my goals and make my dream come true. For the first time in my charmed life, He didn't appear to be on board with my goals and dream.

I was angry. I blamed God and other people for my problems. And when what controlled my life—basketball—had started spiraling out of control, that decision I had made to take control of my happiness, joy, and peace was failing.

Confronted with questions I'd never had to face, I was asking God the wrong question. Instead of asking how God could use me in this situation to reflect His glory in dark times, I was asking why God had allowed the dark times to come in the first place.

12

A DIFFERENT ATMOSPHERE

My new duties as media spokesman began quickly. Two days later, the university held a memorial service for Patrick.

I had never attended a memorial service before. Patrick's girlfriend, an athlete herself, described how much childlike fun Patrick had and how he had helped her learn how to relax and to love. I felt guilty for how selfish I had been all summer, how I had been concerned chiefly with my future in basketball even though the loss of Patrick's life was the tragedy. Three-fourths of the teammates who had been with Patrick were no longer at Baylor, and the few of us who remained mourned his loss.

Afterward, I was taken behind the church to meet with the media. I anticipated a few recognizable reporters with tape recorders. Instead, I took a place standing alone in front of at least ten cameras and more people I did not recognize. Sweat was pouring down the side of my face.

I hoped the questions would be primarily about a new beginning and the future. They weren't.

"Reflecting back, Matt…"

"What do you think about the payments…?"

"Was drug use rampant on the team?"

"Were you aware of…?"

I was sick of this spokesman role, and it had just started. Each time I spoke, I had to be completely focused because any anti-Baylor comments would make matters worse.

A month after Coach Drew came aboard, I still wasn't buying in. "Let's put the summer behind us," he kept telling us. "Let's focus on basketball." But that was impossible for me because the media and students were still asking me about the past.

Coach had told us that many of our roles would change and that increased opportunities on the floor were coming. But I wasn't worried about my skills because basketball was no longer a priority. I had stopped enjoying the sport to which I had devoted basically my entire life. With no postseason to play for, what carrot could they dangle in front of me? Pride? Integrity? The love of playing? I had played for each of those before. But no longer. I had lost all hope.

Before, running around Bear Trail that encircled the campus had been a fun way to get into better shape for basketball, not to mention run into female students! Now that I had been told to work off extra calories, I felt like I was being forced to run. My attitude about the runs had changed.

A few of the assistant coaches, led by Coach Driscoll, ran daily, and I often joined them. We did workouts that today are called "last man sprints." We ran two miles in single file, and the last person in line would sprint to the front. That cycle continued for the entire run. It was a great interval workout that left me exhausted.

The workouts also gave me a chance to get to know the coaches better. While we recovered from a run, they asked me questions about the university. They made sure to steer clear of any talk about the summer.

When I couldn't join the coaches, I worked out on a treadmill in the SLC. Often when I arrived there, Terrance was in the middle of a workout. I was surprised at how much he enjoyed working out. His positivity and optimism were still difficult to figure out, considering how unhappy he had been the previous season. Part of me also wondered if this was Terrance putting on an act or trying to convince himself everything would be okay.

Coach Drew's staff performed their jobs in stark contrast to our previous coaches. The new assistants were creating a family atmosphere that made it comfortable for players to be around them. When the old coaching staff had entered a room, everyone stiffened up. At times, as young as the new coaches were, it was easy to view them as buddies rather than coaches.

I called Coach Driscoll one day to ask if he wanted to join me for a non-mandatory-but-encouraged-for-my-benefit run around Bear Trail.

"Matt, I would," he said, "but I don't think I can get away."

"Come on," I said. "You can squeeze out thirty minutes."

I was pushing on him a little because I did enjoy running with him. He was a great guy who made me feel better about my situation. A few teammates were around me as I continued trying to persuade him.

"Sorry, I just have too much to get done," he said. "But make sure you get your run in."

Almost offended, I shot back, "Come on, man. You know I will get it done."

Awkward silence.

"Are there other players around you?" he asked. He must have heard them in the background.

"Yes."

"Don't talk to me like that in front of other players. Do you understand?"

"Yes, Coach. I understand."

The call ended abruptly.

I had blown past the boundaries of respect. The truth was, I hadn't even seen or felt these boundaries as I flew by. This would have never happened with the previous staff because I would not have dared to feel that comfortable with them. With Coach Drew's staff, the atmosphere was relaxed. Combined with how I viewed our program differently, I had forgotten what was appropriate…and what wasn't. I learned a lesson that I would remember—and teach—for a long time. No matter how close I felt to Coach Driscoll, he was the *coach* and I was the *player*. And that boundary between us could not be crossed.

Oddly, I felt more connected to the coaching staff than my team-mates, which made my workouts feel different.

We had R.T., Will, and Ellis Kidd, a junior who had been a pro-lific scorer in high school. He barely played as a freshman at Oklahoma State and transferred to Baylor. During the season that he was ineligible to play in games, he had flashed spurts of greatness. But he could also be unreliable.

Corey Herring and Tommy Swanson were returning as sophomores but didn't have much on-court experience from their freshman seasons to fall back on. Corey and Harvey Thomas, the forward who sat out the previous season after transferring in from Georgetown, were still a part of the investigation from the summer and awaiting clearance to play.

Our three walk-ons were working hard, but they were walk-ons. Carl, our lone freshman scholarship player, was athletic, but he was still adjusting to the pace of the college game. And then there was Terrance, who, for some reason or another, was more positive than I had ever seen him. He was almost annoying! During the good times, he was upset and whining. But when things couldn't get any worse, he was our best cheerleader? It didn't make sense.

I also knew the coaching staff had a two-year free pass. At least. What pressure were they under? None, as far as wins and losses. They just needed to use us leftovers for this year and the other guys for a few more years to get the stink out of the program. All they needed to do was keep the program from creating more bad headlines and hope people would forget about everything that had happened. *Then* the coaches could get down to serious recruiting. But for now, they had to be on cruise control, didn't they?

I believed the coaches were using me, Terrance, and R.T. I was the illusion. I was the picture of what Baylor was supposed to be, or what I had come to this school for in the first place: a great university athletically and academically, where students were free to display their beliefs. Instead, I was a tool of the establishment. A necessary pawn that would end up as collateral damage. "Thanks for your four years of service to Baylor, and have a nice life. Next!"

My beliefs? I had almost forgotten them by now. When I told my mom that I'd had my first drink on my twenty-first birthday, I disappointed her. She warned me that our family had some heavy drinkers and I needed to be careful. But I wasn't hitting the bottle more than any typical college kid—or so I tried to convince myself.

My view of women also had changed. I hadn't been an angel before, but I also didn't go around breaking hearts. Along with drinking, I was searching for moments of happiness no matter who I had to use to get them. I used to shake my head when my older teammates' stories involved drinking and women. But all my stories now started with, "Well, we were so gone…" or, "Man, I was so smashed…"

One night I decided to attend an FCA meeting on campus. Jess would be there. Our friendship had changed, and I went mainly to keep up the façade that I was still the same guy I had been since we met.

As the worship music started, I could not sing along or at least go through the motions to look good. My chest tightened. A cold sweat broke out. I thought about my relationship with God and how far I had fallen in such a short time. I was still angry at God. *What had I done to deserve this?* I felt convicted and ashamed. I had learned when I was younger that feeling convicted is the Holy Spirit sending you a message. But this moment was too much to take. Without saying a word, I walked past Jess and left. Once outside, I sprinted across campus to my apartment. I had to get these thoughts out of my head. I had to find peace. And if this was God trying to speak to me, then I had to drown Him out.

I started a binge. That would do the trick.

I was handling my problems all wrong. There was no better time for me to call upon God for help, comfort, and refuge. But I refused. I was hurt and stubborn, and I chose to feel sorry for myself. I could have been a shining light but instead wallowed in self-pity in the dark. That remains one of my life's greatest regrets.

A NEW PRESSURE TO PERFORM

One of the fallouts from our program's issues was the establishment of a mandatory drug-testing policy. I had a drug test the morning after the FCA meeting, and although I wasn't worried about failing for drugs, I did fear my hangover could create some type of positive result.

The drive across campus to Robinson Tower offered me time to reflect. We had made it into the NIT in my first season. Now, in my last season, all I seemingly was allowed to do was pee in a cup.

I signed in and showed my school ID. Within a few minutes, two female nurses came in and told me to follow them. A stack of cups sat on a small desk. One nurse took a cup and wrote with a dark marker on the white label, "Sayman, Matt." She handed me the cup and motioned toward the restroom.

"We need you to fill it up, please."

"Okay, sure."

I opened the bathroom door. A single toilet and a small sink were inside. With the empty cup in my right hand, I reached back for the doorknob with my left hand. The door would not close. I tried again, and the door remained stuck. I turned to see the cause of the problem. One of the nurses was holding the door open with her hand and using a foot to block the bottom.

"We need to stay in the room with you," she said.

She had to be kidding, right? Did she think I was going to take out a bag of someone else's urine and squeeze it into the cup?

I wanted to inform the nurses who I was and how long I had played at Baylor. I had done nothing wrong during that time, and they did not need to be in the bathroom with me.

"Are you sure we can all fit in here?" I asked. I could hear my voice rising in panic.

"We do it all the time," one said. "I will stand here, and she will stand there."

The second nurse moved to my left side, by the sink. The lead nurse stood directly behind me.

This is insane! Are you freaking kidding me?

The few times I had been tested during my career, I had entered the bathroom alone. Now there was zero trust, as though I had previously failed a test. Or cheated on one. We were supposed to be focusing on basketball and the future. That is what Coach Drew told us. And here I was in the most uncomfortable position of my life!

I was already talking myself into not being able to pee with two women present. It just wasn't going to happen. I hoped they would leave, and then I could supply them with what they needed.

The room was silent, except for the lead nurse's breathing behind me. Out of the corner of my eye, I saw the nurse to the side staring at me.

Two minutes ticked by. Nothing.

After waiting some more, I suggested going back outside where I could drink water. After I zipped up, I washed my hands. Slowly. That wasted another sixty seconds.

Outside the bathroom, one of the nurses handed me a cup of water. I drank it deliberately, thinking about the difference between a few months earlier and now. Beads of sweat started popping out on my forehead. After a five-minute break, the three of us squeezed back inside the jail cell of a bathroom and tried again.

Five minutes. Nothing.

The nurse to my left reached over and turned on the faucet.

"Here. Maybe running water will help you."

"Yeah, thanks."

Trust me, nothing can help this situation.

Five minutes and what sounded like hundreds of gallons of water went down the drain.

The nurse behind me suggested we step back outside and I drink more water.

I washed my hands again. Then I slowly drank a full glass of cool water. I could not stop telling myself there was no way I would be able to pee in front of women. No way. I just knew they were laughing at me on their insides. *How could they not be?*

We returned to the bathroom. The side nurse turned on the water again.

Two minutes passed.

The nurse behind me suggested we carry on a conversation.

"How has your day been?" she asked.

"Uh, me? My day? Not so good so far. How is *your* day going?"

"Okay," she answered. "It's almost lunchtime, so we are halfway through with the day."

"What sport do you play?" the other asked.

"Basketball," I replied, even though I felt like saying that I used to play basketball but now was part of the circus.

Five more minutes. Still nothing.

The nurses talked to each other while I stood there wishing, begging, pleading for something to happen.

Thirty minutes after first entering the bathroom, I still had an empty cup in my hand. It wasn't like I didn't have a gallon of urine to donate. My now-full bladder eagerly awaited the opportunity to do what it was created to do. But my mind was blocking it from letting go.

Finally, with a lot of focus, it happened. For all the time it took to release, I couldn't get the nurses out of that bathroom fast enough. As soon as they had the full cup, they vanished to allow me to finish in peace.

I walked past them on my way out.

"Sorry."

What else could I say?

"Don't worry," one said. "That happens a lot."

I was utterly embarrassed, even as I rode the elevator alone to the ground floor. And to think, I would have to perform this routine repeatedly because of the school's self-imposed sanctions.

*What was I willing to do to keep playing basketball under these conditions? How far was I willing to go to finish my senior year? Did I **want** to do this?*

The questions terrified me. I had never quit anything in my life. But quitting the sport I had always loved looked like an appealing option.

13

"STAR" BY DEFAULT

Organized practices began on Saturday, October 18. In my previous life, up through my junior year at Baylor, I counted down to the first practice. Now, it was just another day to punch the time clock and keep my scholarship.

Only eleven players were getting dressed in the locker room. I wondered how many drills we could execute with our limited number. I couldn't imagine how difficult of a let's-start-the-season speech this had to be for Coach Drew. What could he say that would inspire us to do everything he needed us to do? What glory could this season offer us?

Coach walked in and wrote "15" on the whiteboard.

"The most important thing this year is your effort," he began. "Baylor deserves your best effort, and the community has to see your best effort. Last year's team won fourteen games. Our goal this year is fifteen wins."

I hoped I had successfully hidden my astonishment. We had won those fourteen games with a complete roster that included two future pros. How in the world could this group of leftovers win more than that team?

Coach explained the rules and policies he expected us to follow. No cursing was allowed in the program—from players, managers, *or* coaches. Coach Bliss would have already broken that rule. Any violation would result in ten pushups on the spot. "We will control what comes out of our mouths," Coach Drew said.

"Second, we will have team Bible studies." Assistant coaches would lead them, he said. I dropped my head. I didn't want any part of those, even though in the past I probably would have volunteered to help run them.

"On that note," he continued, "we will occasionally attend church together."

Coach's final rule was that anything that one person did wrong would result in team punishment. For example, if Ellis missed class, we all would run a Ferrell at 6 a.m. on Sunday. "Running a Ferrell" consisted of running from the floor up each set of steps to the top row of the Ferrell Center and then continuing that pattern all the way around the arena. That was a twenty-minute run, minimum. It was one thing to run a Ferrell in previous seasons when I was putting in extra work to gain an advantage. But it invoked an entirely different mindset to run a Ferrell as punishment for someone else's mistake. Coach Bliss had never punished anyone for a teammate's screwup. When Wendell Greenleaf skipped class or failed a drug test, it didn't affect me.

I'd already had enough of suffering punishment because of others. I wanted to raise my hand and let the coaches know what a bad idea they had.

Then Coach Drew looked at us and smiled. "Finish getting dressed, and I will see you on the floor." His speech could not have been more different from the three preseason speeches I had heard from Coach Bliss.

While we finished dressing out, music started blaring from the arena. It sounded like someone had cued up *Jock Jams, Volume 1*. Seriously?

Terrance grinned and clapped his hands. "Man, let's go!"

I walked through the tunnel to the floor and saw coaches and managers smiling. Some were dancing. All looked excited to get started. I had to wonder whether they had been brainwashed.

When we gathered around midcourt, the music stopped. The coaches and managers outnumbered players.

Coach Drew reminded us of all the things we could not control, like the events of the summer, our limited numbers, and other obstacles we would encounter. We could only control our effort and what we did with the time we had. I appreciated Coach's words, but the truth was that one look around the circle demonstrated that the things we couldn't control were still controlling us.

Paul Mills, an assistant coach, had the word of the day and prayed. Praying before practice was new. I liked Coach Mills. He had been a player, and he talked like a preacher. I did sense the family environment Coach Drew desired to instill, but I remained resistant.

Only a few minutes in, I could see it would take time to get used to how this staff ran practices. After three years with Coach Bliss, I could have planned out a practice for him, and he probably would have followed it.

We started with a defensive zig-zag progression that ended with us playing full-court one-on-one. Our bodies weren't loose yet, so some of us were not going full speed. I told Coach Driscoll we weren't loose and asked, "How can we go full speed?"

"When a dog is lying down and sees a car go by," he answered, "he immediately starts chasing it. The dog doesn't need to stretch." Then he grinned.

I was probably a little too sensitive, but I didn't appreciate the comparison to what a dog does.

Coach Drew blew his whistle and, with intensity, yelled, "You can't get the last fifteen minutes back! Don't waste the next fifteen."

I ended practice tired and frustrated. In the locker room, Coach Drew announced that after we cleaned up, we would meet with a team psychologist. Our guest seemed harmless, but I doubted that Kansas and Texas were wrapping up their first day like that.

We met the psychologist in a room with chairs set in a circle. I envisioned eleven D-I players holding hands and singing "Kumbaya." My guard was fully up, and the disapproving expressions on several teammates' faces made me feel better.

The doctor came across as a nice man, but he immediately alienated me by using young people's lingo, as though he was trying to be one of us. He wanted us to talk about any pain or emotion we still carried from the scandal. I wanted to ask him which one he wanted to hear about first because I had a list. Patrick's death? Being betrayed by a coach? Losing ten teammates? The difficulty of living in a community that looked at us as though *we* were the criminals and rule-breakers?

One by one, teammates began expressing their difficulties with our situation. How it made them feel. Most of them had not been here more than a year. I wanted to yell at them to stop complaining because none of them had been there as long as I had. Terrance and R.T. had some right to speak, but they also remained quiet. If the three of us weren't going to whine, then no one should.

No competitive, self-respecting program was having this discussion. We were going to be the laughingstock of Division I.

After a wasted hour, I couldn't wait to get a drink.

UNPOPULAR ON CAMPUS

ESPN's *Outside the Lines* wanted to air a story on Coach Drew and what it was like on our campus post-tragedy, and I was asked to participate in an interview. Being on a highly watched program like *Outside the Lines* wasn't the cool opportunity it would probably seem to most.

ESPN wasn't coming to Baylor because we were on the cusp of success and everyone wanted to be a part of it. They hadn't requested to interview me because I was the stud player on a team expected to make a splash in this year's NCAA Tournament. I was being interviewed as a leftover, and the oldest leftover at that. I was a "star" player by default. But I continued doing the same dance I had been doing and agreed to the interview.

When the show aired, I saw firsthand how our student body felt. Students had been treating me and approaching me differently. The distance between "us" and "them" had grown. The looks I noticed had changed from "He's an athlete" to "There's a troublemaker." One interviewee said that when a friend learned he attended Baylor, he was warned to watch out for "those basketball players." Another shared her frustration that people viewed her differently as a student because of our program. *Had she lost teammates? Had her coach betrayed her? What did she have to be so offended about?* She added it had been bad enough having the ties between Waco and Branch Davidians cult leader David Koresh. And now Baylor basketball too?

All the students who looked differently at us were still able to go to class and function normally. They weren't reminded daily of what they had lost. I was. Did anyone care about how I felt?

Coach Drew handled his interview well. The whole country was able to see what we experienced every day. He was impressive with his energy and optimism. He made it believable that he saw enormous opportunity in the program. In a different circumstance, on a different team, I would have loved to play for a guy like Coach Drew.

Outside the Lines host Bob Ley asked Coach the key questions: Will recruiting be difficult? How will his coaching staff be able to tell a parent that their son would be safe coming to Baylor?

We knew what had occurred was an isolated incident and that everyone directly involved was gone. But I imagined the rest of the country viewed us leftovers as thugs not to be trusted.

Coach Drew told Ley that when recruits visited the campus, took in its beauty, and met the quality people there, in time, they would come. Coach described a Baylor that I once believed in but no longer saw. I missed that Baylor.

"THAT PLAYER"

Our numbers made practices difficult. Injuries or players held out of practice over ongoing investigation-related matters could prevent us from having any realistic five-on-five situations. Coach Drew came up with an idea to add bodies. He scheduled an open walk-on tryout from within the student body that would offer students the opportunity to cheer for one of their own.

In other words, someone who was sitting in the seats watching us play last year could now be on the court playing with us. Our desperation frustrated me. And our Big 12 opponents had to be laughing.

The tryout took place on October 20. Our first exhibition game was fifteen days away, and here Coach Driscoll was putting students through drills while Coach Drew looked on from the stands, pad and pen in hand. I was asked to attend and show my support. A cameraman for *Inside Baylor Sports* came to me sitting on the sideline and asked my take on the tryout. I pointed to the court and said, "I like him. He's really athletic." I was pointing to a blank space on the floor. Out of the fifty or so guys who showed up, I didn't think any could help us.

Robbie McKenzie won the contest. I had played against him at the SLC. At six-five, he was the best, most athletic player in the tryout.

More importantly, Robbie was a good guy. If nothing else, he was pre-med and would make us look better. Still, he was an undersized post player, and I knew the quality of athletes he would be going up against in conference games. I questioned whether the tryout was a publicity stunt. This new player would give the student body something to get excited about when the "one of their own" walk-on entered the game late in blowout losses.

Robbie made the team in time for our annual Midnight Madness, a kickoff-type event that gave the Baylor and Waco communities a preview of the products the men's and women's programs would put on the floor that season. I wasn't sure if anyone would show up this year.

Two teammates and I competed in a three-point shooting contest against the women's team. Luckily, we won, although coming close to losing was embarrassing.

Jess was a senior for the Lady Bears, and their program was precisely where I had dreamed our team would be my senior year. They were the Baylor team the university would hope could produce a deep postseason run. Not us leftovers.

My apartment had become known as the site for good parties, and Jess obviously did not attend any of them. I could tell she didn't understand why I had changed, and seeing her again, I wanted to explain that I was searching for relief. For even just a little bit of peace. The only way I could find relief and peace was to numb myself for a few hours. But I knew Jess would want to point me to another source for strength. The right one.

Terrance was amazing during Midnight Madness, smiling and laughing throughout. He had transformed into a Baylor-first, me-second guy…and I did not know why. During the dunk contest, he grabbed the mic and hyped up the crowd. He danced up into the stands, and the fans responded by jumping out of their seats and dancing along. I smiled at how much fun Terrance was having.

Harvey and Ellis wowed the crowd with their dunking abilities, and then everyone stood for our school song, "That Good Old Baylor Line." I stood with right hand raised in our "Sic 'Em" bear claw signal meant to display school spirit as the fans sang together:

That good old Baylor Line

That good old Baylor Line

We'll march forever down the years

As long as stars shall shine

We'll fling our Green and Gold afar

To light the ways of time

And guide us as we onward go

That good old Baylor Line

I had not heard our school song since the last home game of my junior season. Even though I held my "Sic 'Em" high like the others, my chin was lowered and my eyes locked in on the floor. *Could I do this for five more months?*

The following Sunday, I was halfway up Section 204 at the Ferrell Center when I felt the need to throw up. It was 6:30 in the morning. I had stopped drinking around 3 a.m. I was in no condition to run a Ferrell, but one of our teammates had skipped class, so everyone suffered the consequences.

I slowed my pace a bit so I wouldn't vomit and then almost tripped on a stair. My Ferrell took thirty minutes to complete. Then it was to the showers to get cleaned up for church.

We loaded into SUVs for the ride and were passing around boxes of doughnuts when a foreign object smashed into our windshield. The guys in the SUV ahead of us were launching jelly-filled doughnuts at us. It was so on! We drove up next to them and fired back. This was the most fun I'd had while sober in a long time. None of the coaches attempted to stop us, as if they were happy we were starting to gel.

On Tuesday, I had lunch with Terrance at a Quiznos. I was behind in fulfilling Coach Drew's request to meet with each team member because I was resisting my leadership role. I had come to tolerate doing my part with the media, but I hadn't made it a high priority to spend my personal time trying to help unite the team when winning or losing didn't matter.

Terrance and I had switched roles. He had embraced change. I wondered, though, if privately, he struggled the same as me.

As we talked over our sandwiches, I felt Terrance persuading me that there was hope for the season. It was almost like Coach Drew had asked Terrance to meet with me and get me on board, not vice versa. Terrance said he believed in Coach Drew, which almost made me laugh considering how he had feuded with the coach I had believed in. Our conversation hammered home just how drastically our roles had reversed.

Terrance gave me a hug and a huge smile outside Quiznos.

Just wait, I thought. *Once we start getting smashed by teams, we'll see if he is still smiling.*

Later that week, I was headed to meet some of the guys at Cricket's and decided to drop the top down on my Mustang and drive through campus. I went down South Eighth Street past Common Grounds, a popular coffee hangout for students. As I turned toward the highway, a billboard caught my eye. I circled the car around and pulled into a Kwik Stop parking lot. I got out of my car and walked toward the street.

The billboard was an advertisement for our team, with action shots of three players. Terrance was sprinting down the court with a ball. R.T. was in the middle, releasing a shot. The third senior seemed to have a fire in his eyes. You could tell that when he played, he played with passion. He was dribbling a ball with his right hand while directing players on the court with his left as he yelled instructions. It was the old me, the "Baylor first, me second" Bear.

I was embarrassed the school was advertising for this new season. *Come see the group of leftovers who can't play in any postseason contests and probably wouldn't be good enough to do so anyway!*

I got back into my car and hurried away. I couldn't imagine myself being that player again.

14

LET THE GAMES BEGIN

I had just finished lacing up my shoes when, out of the corner of my eye, I noticed a teammate sipping from a bottle that looked odd. I took a closer look. He was drinking a wine cooler. In the locker room!

I asked him, "What are you doing?"

He downed the rest of the drink and shook his head.

"Man, can't smoke weed anymore," he explained. "Gotta do something."

Our new drug-testing policies presented a challenge for the guys who smoked marijuana. That's how far our program had fallen. Of course, I would be drinking later that night. We each did what we could to get by. But at least I wasn't drinking in the locker room. The crazy thing was that with the wine cooler consumed, my teammate turned in the best practice I had seen from him.

Our first exhibition game was the next day against the Raiders Select, a team from Australia. These touring teams typically consisted of former college and semipro players paid to come in and get beat up on by the host team as dress rehearsals for the games that counted. I was nervous that this season, we might be the team that suffered the pounding.

Coach Drew had installed an offense centered on a concept called "idiot motion." Because we would be outmanned each night, we needed to minimize the number of possessions in each game. Our goal was to milk the thirty-five-second shot clock time on each possession by executing idiot motion, which meant screening and cutting like chickens with their heads cut off until about fifteen seconds left to shoot. At that point, Carl or I would get the ball and initiate a set play. I understood the need for this slower style of play, but I hated it.

I had loved being part of a motion offense that allowed us to work until we found the best option for a shot. I excelled in that type of system. But in idiot motion, it was like our brains had been switched off.

Under Coach Bliss, we had played a solid man-to-man pressure defense, at times throwing in our "Bear Trap" 1-3-1 zone with an athletic guard or forward at the top. I loved scouting opponents' game film to see how I would need to maneuver through the other team's plays and learn how to effectively guard superior players. Now, we were employing a standard 2-3 zone, except our top guards started in a tandem with one in front of the other.

Carl proved helpful in this defense because I was in my worst shape ever and needed to rest often on defense. On the opponent's first pass, I was supposed to go guard the ball, allowing Carl to watch the high post area. Because Carl listened to everything I told him and possessed endless energy, I told him to follow the ball instead. There were possessions when I stood in one spot while Carl chased the ball all over the perimeter. I figured my way was okay because no one told us to do it differently.

Our coaches were in their offices by 8 a.m. and sometimes worked until 11 p.m. They were constantly on their phones, working contacts to identify recruits who could lift the program out of the murk. One of their targeted players was Aaron Bruce, a guard on our first exhibition opponent. He apparently was close to giving his commitment to play at Baylor. By playing against us, he would see that getting playing time would not be a problem here.

The NCAA had yet to clear Corey or Harvey to play, leaving us with six scholarship players and four walk-ons against the Australians. On the day of the exhibition, Coach Drew surprised us by unveiling new uniforms. They looked great, except for being from a foreign brand I had never heard of. I guessed Nike or Adidas didn't want to be associated with our program either.

As a freshman, holding my number 13 jersey for the first time and reading "SAYMAN" across the back had signaled my arrival in big-time college basketball. On this day, I turned my new jersey around. The space above my number was blank. I assumed a mistake had been made.

Coach Drew explained the lack of last names on our jerseys to us: "The name on the front is more important than the one on the back."

I had heard coaches say that many times. My "me monster" raged. After three seasons, I had earned the right to have my name on my jersey for my senior year. After all, I stayed when most of the others didn't!

We returned to the locker room after pregame shoot-around to a party with music blaring from the sound system. Coach Tang was banging a metal trashcan with a drumstick. Coaches and managers were clapping and dancing. I thought I had walked into a club, not a pregame speech. Under Bliss, we were quiet and focused at this time, ready for our leader to address us and make sure we knew our assignments. This atmosphere seemed more like a distraction than anything else. However, I noticed a few of the other players were getting into the scene.

Then Coach Drew started talking. He said our areas of focus needed to be limiting turnovers and good shot selection. More importantly, our effort must be constant. I felt like Coach Drew was talking to me alone.

I had always enjoyed my pregame jitters, regardless of the level of ball. They were almost like a drug. But before our first exhibition under our new coaches, I was anxious.

The opening jump ball—the first action of the season—sent the ball bouncing toward the scorer's table. These had been my moments to demonstrate my willingness to do anything for the team. Trying to keep the ball inbounds, I launched my body over the scorer's table and heard the usual extra applause I received for such plays. This time, I didn't feel the same satisfaction as in previous seasons. This scorer's table leap seemed forced.

We weren't even out of our first preseason game when our depth issue revealed itself. Tommy got into early foul trouble, and R.T. tweaked an ankle. At one point, we had two walk-ons on the court together. If that happened in the Big 12 schedule, blood would be shed.

I played thirty-seven of the forty minutes, and Ellis played thirty-five. I had not played so much in a game since I was a sophomore and in phenomenal shape. My body ached like I had run a marathon.

We won 83–73, and Coach Drew was pleased with our effort. But still, I sensed some legitimate concern in the locker room. This was an exhibition against mostly older guys, some of whom had played at our level. No need to worry about Big 12 opponents yet—what would happen when we started our nonconference games? A newspaper article printed some time ago stated that we might not win a game all season. I believed some of us feared that could be true.

I was cleaning up, still a little winded, when Heath made his familiar locker room appearance to collect players for the postgame news conference. This season, I couldn't hide. I released a heavy sigh and headed to the press room.

Sure enough, the first question started with, "Matt, reflecting back over the summer..."

THERE'S ONE!

Baylor's athletic program wasn't then what it is today. There wasn't a lot of pride in our teams except for baseball and tennis, although I could see that coach Kim Mulkey was building the women's basketball program to where it would be a perennial contender for the conference championship—and more. The last time our football team had produced a winning season, I was in junior high. Now, our program seemed to be adding to the gloom. No chance at the postseason and not a lot of pride in place, either. What were we playing for?

After drilling some team called World HoopStars 104–38 in our second exhibition game—having a lot of much-needed fun in the process—we finally received one piece of good news regarding our roster: Corey was cleared to play, giving us seven scholarship players for our regular-season opener against Texas Southern.

Following the pregame jam session by our coaches and managers in the locker room, Terrance and Ellis were upbeat. Our team chaplain, Pastor Mark Wible, spoke about David taking on Goliath from 1 Samuel 17 in the Old Testament. David volunteered to fight to the death against the opposing army's giant warrior. The winning army would enslave the loser's people. With no armor, sword, or shield, David marched into battle armed with only a slingshot and five smooth stones. His first and only shot found Goliath's forehead, the giant's lone vulnerable spot. Goliath crumpled to the ground, and David took Goliath's sword and cut off his opponent's head. Victory!

According to the chaplain, we would be just like David. I struggled to accept his analogy. Our recently-snapped official team photo would go into Baylor's history books as the team with more coaches and managers than players. What kind of stone could we hurl at Texas? At

Kansas? The Oklahoma team that had blasted us and our full roster? Goliath was going to smack David around this season.

I led our team out of the tunnel to a Ferrell Center with more than half of the 10,000-plus seats unclaimed. The pregame energy we had become accustomed to feeling from our fans was missing from the arena.

We wore black strips on our jerseys in remembrance of Patrick and held a moment of silence before that game to honor him. These were both appropriate gestures, but everywhere we played, people would be reminded of what had happened. We had been told the summer was over and we could move on because of hope in the future. Yet even doing the right things forced us to retreat into the past.

Although Texas Southern was D-I, it played in a mid-major conference. Our previous teams would have won this game handily.

Our starters' talent advantage allowed us to jump out to a big early lead that we maintained until almost halfway through the second half. Then fatigue and foul trouble hit us, and Texas Southern went on an 18–4 run that cut our lead to eight points with eight minutes left. The lead and the game were slipping away. I noticed that the coaches' use of the walk-ons dropped dramatically the rest of the game. We held on to win 72–59—not the pounding we should have delivered, but still a win.

The scholarship players were gassed. I played thirty-seven minutes, Terrance played thirty-six, and R.T. and Ellis each played thirty-four. The dominant feeling in the locker room was relief. At least we would no longer have to answer the question about whether we would win a game.

One down, fourteen to go to reach Coach's goal. A few of the guys appeared emboldened by the victory. I started hearing talk about how we would win *more* than fifteen games. But I knew how long of a ride a season is from beginning to end.

FOLLOWING THE WRONG PATH

The following Monday evening, I was racing through my apartment, picking up trash. The team Bible study that coaches Mills and Tang tag-teamed to run was coming to my place. And I had forgotten. I scooped up the beer cans and shot glasses strewn around the place. I opened the windows and liberally applied air freshener to anything not moving, hoping to remove the cigar stench. Getting my apartment cleaned in time took some *real* hustle!

Coach Mills led this study. We opened our Bibles, but I was distracted by the dread someone would find a beer cap in a couch cushion. Not to mention the guilt over sitting with my coaches and teammates diving into Scripture while feeling the need to apologize for the lingering smell from the previous night's party.

Coach Mills grabbed my attention when he said, "Some guys, they think they can party now in college and get back into their faith when they get out of school. Like, 'After I get out of college, then I will slow down.' If that's you, you're so wrong. The temptations are still going to be there when you get out. And your habits in college will carry over. And it may even be harder to quit then."

I was so arrogant that I almost blurted out, "That's exactly what I am going to do." I had lived God's way before. No reason why I couldn't do so again when I was ready. For now, I would do whatever I needed to do to make it through this pain, and then when I was away from Baylor, I would get back to church and straighten up.

On the day of the Texas Southern game, our athletics website had published a feature article on me titled "Leader of Men." In the article, Coach Drew called me "steady and reliable." His concluding words were, "Everything Matt does is at 100 percent." He hadn't seen my 100 percent! I didn't believe he ever would.

Robbie, our new walk-on, was quoted as saying that I never complained. Reading what he and Coach said about me was embarrassing.

But more troublesome was one of my own quotes: "Push yourself, and when you have done all that you can, leave the rest to God."

Pathetic. And hypocritical. I was talking one way and living the opposite.

PREPARING FOR THE MONSTER

Our winning streak to start the season lasted one game. Another team from a mid-major conference, Stephen F. Austin State University, came to Waco right before Thanksgiving and defeated us by twenty-two. We couldn't get into any kind of offensive rhythm, and I made only two of my ten shots. After one of my questionable shot choices, I heard the crowd groan.

I recognized the team needed me to score, but I hadn't played that role since high school. I was stressing out on the court. Growing up, although the game was played at a fast pace, I could mentally see options unfolding one after the other until I chose the correct one. Now, I felt lost and useless.

Ellis and Terrance tried to encourage me after the game.

I snapped, "I can't see anything out there!" My throat closed, and my eyes started filling with tears. I had never experienced this uncertainty in basketball.

Over the years, I'd had a group of fans who had supported me no matter what…and another group who couldn't understand how I made it to the D-I level. The second group never bothered me. I knew how hard I had worked and what value I brought to my team. But now, I was interested in what our fans were saying about me.

With a beverage in hand, I checked out the message boards at baylorfans.com. I'd mainly had support from the fans there, but they were turning against me. I read anonymous fans asking why I was shooting so much when I wasn't hitting anything. I couldn't argue with that. They also were puzzled how I made it to Baylor's level.

Some suggested I sit down and allow the walk-ons to play more. I took their comments personally because, unlike others, I had stayed and was playing for these fans.

I leaned back and stared at the ceiling. I wished I knew the fans' identities so I could address them. They didn't know what I had been through and how miserable I was. But I did know that a lot of people didn't think I should be at Baylor. At least we had that in common.

We were 3–2 heading into a game at North Texas—we had sandwiched defeats of Texas A&M-Corpus Christi and Midwestern State around a tough loss to SMU. I continued to be ineffective on the floor, and my effort was not great in practices or games. Terrance was consistent with his attitude on and off the court and led us in scoring most games. Ellis was picking up the slack when it looked like no one else would step up.

Most of the scholarship players were logging significant minutes. Sometimes during games, our team appeared to be heading in the right direction, only to have fatigue set in.

For our first road trip, Coach Drew took us to Denton the day before the game. Under Coach Bliss, I had been allowed to pick my roommates on the road, so I chose guys with whom I would be comfortable. Coach Drew assigned me to room with Joe Simmons.

Joe was a football player who had joined our team as a walk-on. He must have watched our early games and saw a chance for playing time. We needed all the bodies we could bring on board. Joe was a nice guy, but at bedtime, he was talking to his girlfriend on the phone. Not for ten minutes. Not for an hour. They talked until 4 a.m. I didn't know Joe that well yet, plus he was a massive defensive lineman—six-five, 250 pounds—so I didn't say anything to him about keeping me awake. At one point, I went out into the hallway to read. This was not how I preferred my pregame nights to unfold.

When Coach Drew asked why I was so sleepy-eyed on game day, I told him what had happened. He was not happy.

In basketball, you get used to fans yelling at you on the road. At Missouri, fans shouted at me that they didn't know *NSYNC was in town. I must have had a boy band look to me. At least they weren't nasty. We had a married player, and at Texas Tech, fans had looked up his wife's name and made *extremely* inappropriate remarks about her all night. John Lucas's father was well known for overcoming substance abuse and forming a recovery program for athletes, so John was tormented about his dad's drug problem all the time, often starting pregame from a fan courtside. I liked John's solution: when the loudmouth wasn't looking during warmups, he rifled a pass right at the fan's head to get their attention.

The UNT fans called us murderers and accused us of being paid to play. UNT was about forty miles from my home, and my family and friends had come to the game. It was difficult for my mom to hear her son called a murderer.

Except for R.T. and Terrance, we played flat in the first half. Terrance was the only one shooting well. With us down by four at halftime, Coach Drew was disgusted with the lack of effort. "The first three minutes of this half are really important," he told us. "We need to come out hard and make a stand." This was a moment in the past when I would jump and shout encouragement. I stayed silent.

UNT started the second half by nailing three three-pointers and took a fourteen-point lead. But Ellis started a 17–1 run for us, and then he hit a three to tie the score at 50. When Terrance made a layup to give us a 52–50 lead, we looked like we might pick up a road win.

At one point, I looked to the sideline and saw Coach Tang with our walk-ons clapping and chanting "Defense!" Robbie had proved wrong my suspicion that his tryout was a PR stunt. The other walk-ons weren't playing much, but they were constantly positive and vocally supporting the team.

Ellis and Terrance were the only reasons we were in the game, and I couldn't seem to do anything to help them. I made an aggressive drive and tried to loft a floater over one of UNT's athletic centers. He swatted the ball clear to half-court like a volleyball player, setting up one of his teammates for an easy dunk.

A year earlier, we beat UNT by twenty-six. On this night, we lost by four, 73–69. I was impressed by the never-quit attitude in some of the guys. Ellis continued to be a bright spot and led us in times when we needed a leader. Terrance and I logged thirty-eight minutes each, but his were far more productive. At this point in the season, considering my lack of production, it didn't make sense for the coaches to play me as much as they were.

The quiet bus ride home reflected the disappointment of a missed opportunity to snatch a victory. Who knew if that would be our last such opportunity?

15

LINE IN THE SAND

One of the beauties of basketball is that after a disappointing loss like ours at North Texas, it's usually only a few days until you get a chance to correct your mistakes. Lose in football and it's a week, sometimes two, before you can try to get back on track. Even the four days until the University of Texas-San Antonio came to face us at the Ferrell Center seemed like a long time to make amends for losing at UNT.

I admired Terrance not only for how well he was playing but also his attitude. He was our leading scorer and captured our fans' hearts by showing his. The difference between Terrance and me was that he had made a wise choice when he opened his eyes to see the opportunities that arrived with the new coaching staff. I made poor choices. Going against everything I was taught about facing adversity, I decided to run—run to things like alcohol and casual female encounters that I was warned were deceptive in their ability to bring relief.

My normal had changed with scary speed. Activities I would not have considered taking part in a year ago were part of my everyday routine. My "poor me" attitude had blinded me to the same opportunities Terrance was enjoying.

During some alone time, I reflected on the Old Testament story of Moses and Joshua in the book of Numbers, chapters 13 and 14. Moses was leading the nation of Israel to the Promised Land, and he sent twelves spies ahead to survey the land of Canaan. Ten returned and reported that although what God had promised about the land was true, the people living there were too strong and their cities too fortified for Israel to overtake. The other two spies, Caleb and Joshua, disagreed, saying Israel would be victorious because God was on their side. But Moses listened to the majority and, as a result, Israel wandered in the desert for forty years. After Moses died, Joshua succeeded him, led Israel in its conquest of Canaan, and both he and Caleb were able to live in the Promised Land.

Like Moses, I had a trust problem with God. Despite all the good Moses had achieved, he was not allowed to see his dream fulfilled because he did not trust in God when he received the spies' scouting report. I felt like I too had come close to realizing my dream but would not see it come true.

The burden of living my way took me to my basketball rock bottom after the UTSA game.

The Roadrunners had lost four games in a row. With Terrance and Ellis on their rolls, we would have an early advantage when our starting five was on the floor. Playing at home also would provide us a confidence boost. Our biggest question was the one we faced every game: how long could our legs carry us?

So much for that early advantage and confidence boost.

We shot 20 percent and were outrebounded 28–16 in the first half. At halftime, UTSA led 28–16. Players can feel the crowd's collective emotions during a game, and our fans had grown increasingly impatient with us.

Clear and simple, those of us playing the most minutes were not producing. In the past, I felt an urgency to make a positive contribution when I substituted into the game because I knew Coach Bliss would not hesitate to pull me. Our teams then had capable players hungry to grab anyone's minutes they could.

Coach Drew ripped into us at halftime. It was our first blistering under him, and we deserved it. Coach questioned why we weren't playing harder and why we weren't taking advantage of this opportunity to get a win. As he ripped us, I wondered, *Who is he going to sub in for me? There is no one else.*

So much for the halftime blistering helping us too.

In the first four minutes of the second half, UTSA stretched its lead to 35–19. Coach Drew called timeout to get us off the floor as quickly as possible. By the time I made it to our sideline, Coach had already huddled the five walk-ons and was giving them instructions. The floor was theirs, the bench was ours. I couldn't believe he was putting five walk-ons in together. I took my seat, thinking, *Good luck. Let's see how this turns out.*

Our crowd instantly applauded its approval of benching the starters.

On the walk-ons' first possession, Will Allen snagged an offensive rebound and finished for the bucket. The subs were flying around on the defensive end and got a stop. Their urgency showed as they advanced the ball up the court. Will launched a deep three from the right wing. Nothing but net. There were fewer than 4,000 people in the Ferrell Center, but everyone was on their feet. Ryan Pryor waved his hands as he sprinted back on defense, urging the fans to cheer even louder. They did.

The subs had cut our deficit to eleven. The crowd was going crazy. Then UTSA's scholarship players asserted themselves.

Coach Drew looked down the bench to us starters and told us, "You better play hard."

We jogged back onto the floor, slapping the walk-ons' hands and congratulating their effort. Then I heard an unfamiliar sound. Boos filled the Ferrell Center. The crowd didn't want us back in the game. I stood at center court, looking up into the seats in both disbelief and anger. I had played in some great games here, and these fans had once adored me. R.T., Terrance, Ellis, Tommy, and I had chosen to stay at Baylor. And this was our thanks? I wanted to scream at the fans. Or at least give them a nonverbal gesture to let them see how I felt about them at this moment. I didn't stay at Baylor for this.

I wasn't the only irritated starter. We ripped off a 16–4 run to close within two points with 2:39 left. But we could get no closer and lost 53–45. We had lost the game and our fans.

TIME TO MAKE A DECISION

Coach Drew stared at us in the locker room until he broke the silence to thank the walk-ons for their effort. "Tonight was a winnable game for us," he said. "And for some of you to not give your best effort is inexcusable."

I kept looking at the floor. I had the feeling that if I looked up, I would see Coach looking directly at me. I was so filled with anger and bitterness that I thought I would explode. The other players quickly dressed and vacated the locker room. I stayed at my locker, still wearing my jersey. Eventually, I made my way to the shower.

I turned on the water, and six months of emotion and grief overwhelmed me. I slumped to the shower floor. I had never been much of a crier, but tears flowed. Coach Driscoll walked into the doorway. I no longer cared to hide what a mess I had become. With water running over me, I looked up at Coach.

"I don't think I can do this," I said.

I had never quit anything in my life. Even in seventh grade, when I had started on the swim team and quickly realized I had no desire to keep competing, my mom made me finish the season. But now, quitting seemed like my only way out. Besides, our own fans had made it known they didn't want me. It's not like it would matter if I quit.

Coach Driscoll listened as I released my frustrations. He did not tell me to snap out of it or say I was acting foolish. When I finished, he calmly told me, "Let's just take it one day at a time, and we will figure this out tomorrow."

The walk-ons were a big hit, and fans were affectionately calling them the "hit squad." Coach Drew's decision to put five walk-ons on the floor together was praised as his best move yet. Although I was happy the guys were seeing their hard work recognized, the praise being heaped on them stung.

The next day's practice started like all the others. I was paired with Carl, the freshman point guard. Athletically, he could run circles around me. But I had him on size and experience. On this day, he was extra annoying with how much he was putting his hands all over me when he guarded me. Still carrying frustration from the night before, I resorted to shoving Carl with both hands as I moved around the court. Coach Tang encouraged Carl to respond by getting more physical with me. I ordinarily loved this type of competition, but I wanted no part in it.

Coach Drew had some running for us to do as a reminder that anything less than our best effort was not good enough. Coach Thomas loved to employ these types of reminders. Coach Bliss had me thinking plenty of times that I was about to lose my lunch. I had been put through these punishment runs on countless occasions. But I did not want to run this time. What good would extra running do us? It didn't matter if we won or lost. There would be no postseason. I still hadn't come up with a good reason to keep playing.

On each sprint, I was last to finish and after the coach's whistle. That meant more punishment that would continue until every player finished before the whistle. In the past, I would have lit into a teammate for making the rest of us keep running, especially if that player wasn't running to his capability. My teammates still respected me, so even though I'm sure they were annoyed after each rep I missed, none said anything to me. Until one decided he'd had enough.

I heard someone say, "You're supposed to be a leader."

I turned to see who was calling me out. It was Turner Phipps, the cocky, unrealistic, freshman walk-on who during the summer thought he would work his way into playing time under Coach Bliss.

"Shut up!" Terrance yelled at Turner.

I said nothing. I wasn't upset at Turner, just embarrassed. I didn't need this. The time had come to decide whether I would be on board or not. Straddling the line wasn't helping me or the team.

After practice, when everyone had left the locker room, I pulled out the UTSA game film. In high school, I had become a fan of watching film postgame because, as coaches love to say, the film doesn't lie. It reveals where you're good and where you need more work. This season, I hadn't watched any film outside of what we watched with our coaches.

I pressed play. I saw a shell of the player I had been. I didn't observe open defiance, and to an untrained eye, there probably wasn't much to notice. And it wasn't necessarily what I was doing wrong with my playing time—it was that I wasn't doing *all I could* with my time. I saw no fire or desire. Nothing about how I played made me think, "That number 13 gets it."

I shifted my focus to my teammates and coaches. They had something I was missing—especially Terrance. He had transformed into the leader I was expected to be this season. My teammates were playing with effort. I watched the walk-ons inspire the crowd with how hard they worked. Tommy and Corey, though inexperienced, were bringing great energy, and their athleticism allowed them to compete against anyone. Ellis and Terrance were scoring consistently. Carl was fitting in nicely and adjusting well to Coach Drew's system. R.T. was as dependable as ever, producing precisely as he was capable. Harvey was expected to be cleared any day now, and his presence would be a shot of adrenaline to our team.

And then there was our new staff. Coaches Driscoll, Tang, and Mills were constant encouragers on the bench, and they spent most of their time out of their seats. Coach Drew was working hard in coaching this bunch of leftovers. Winning games mattered to him. He had said he was bringing us hope. But hope in what? Whether these guys meant it or not, they at least looked like they cared.

What was holding me back? I wasn't walking on the court, cussing people out, getting hit with technical fouls, or not playing somewhat hard. But I wasn't giving everything I was capable of giving. Those close to me saw it. Turner saw I wasn't the leader I was supposed to be, and he had the stuff to call me out when others didn't. Turner had unknowingly forced me into a decision.

I had never quit anything in my life—and I wouldn't now. No one was promising glory or guaranteeing success, but I had to get on board with these guys.

16

DISCOVERING
NEW PERSPECTIVES

I wasn't naïve enough to believe my attitude change would turn our season around.

It wasn't like my teammates were waiting for me to get on board with them so we could run off a winning streak. They understood what it would take to make this season a success. But at least caring and giving my maximum effort would allow me to feel pride in playing again.

We had a 3–4 record in mid-December. Six nonconference games remained. Then we would start Big 12 play, where we were not expected to win a game. The math looked bad for reaching Coach's goal of fifteen wins. Of course, the argument could have been made that the math looked bad at the start of the season.

We needed to reevaluate our goal.

No one expected us to be competitive in games, much less win. So our goal would be to be competitive. Because we could not play in the postseason, each game on our schedule would be our championship game. We would show anyone who was watching that we were competitors to be respected.

The University of Louisiana at Monroe was our first opportunity to pursue our new goal.

Coach Drew called a team meeting before our pregame walk-through. He was struggling to tell us something.

"We are going to be moving on without Ellis," he said.

The locker room was silent.

"He violated a team policy, and we will not be going into it any further."

Losing any player off a twelve-man roster caused problems, but Ellis wasn't just any player with his 13.4 points and four rebounds per game. Plus, he was a good teammate, always cheerful with his great sense of humor.

With Coach's announcement, we dropped from seven to six scholarship players. We were waiting for Harvey to receive clearance to play, and he would be a big boost, but we had twenty-two games in front of us, and a majority of us were spending hours in the training room receiving treatment. My old neck injury had been flaring up, and I had days when it hurt too much to turn my neck. My mom believed my emotional stress was affecting me physically. She might have been correct.

Coach started Carl at point guard, which allowed me to move to the two. I welcomed the switch because bringing the ball up the court against smaller, quicker guys every possession had been wearing me out.

ULM used its depth to its advantage in giving us all we could handle early. Throughout the first half, neither team led by more than six points. Coach inserted the hit squad early in the second half. The crowd roared its approval, and this time I jogged to the bench appreciative of a much-needed break. The walk-ons' energy was inspiring again even though they didn't score in their four minutes in the game. When we subbed back in, our crowd let the subs know how much they appreciated their effort. Thankfully, our fans didn't boo our return to the court.

Even though Terrance was having a monster game in every way, the margin stayed close. Fittingly for the effort both teams were giving, the game went into overtime after ULM hit a three-pointer with eleven seconds left in regulation.

"We ain't losing this game!" Terrance barked. Everyone in our team huddle nodded. We could have put ULM away with free throws, but we missed three out of four. Our legs were gone, and it showed at the free throw line. With the score tied in the final seconds, I shot a three-pointer for the win. The ball sailed long, and R.T.'s attempt at a tip-in at the buzzer came up short.

Oh, boy. Five *more* minutes!

Carl knocked down two clutch free throws to put us up four, and with twenty-two seconds left in the second overtime, Terrance was trapped by a double-team. T made an unbelievable, fifty-foot underhand pass to Corey underneath the basket, and Corey's layup secured an 85–79 victory.

Amid our celebration, I looked up to my parents into the stands. For the first time that season, I saw joy on their faces.

Terrance, R.T., Carl, and I all played at least forty-three minutes. My stats weren't great, but I was back to doing the little things that were important to my game. I loved being part of this win.

The locker room scene didn't match our 4–4 record. We were hugging and chest-bumping each other.

"You refused to lose!" Coach told us. "You never stopped trying, and for that, I am truly proud."

Coach Drew's father, the longtime Valparaiso coach, was at the game. I was so happy he could see not only an exciting victory but also the impact his son was making on our community—and a bunch of leftovers.

TEAM BONDING

I hosted the postgame party at my apartment. We knew we would pay for our celebration in the morning, but we were willing to accept that. Terrance, R.T., and I bonded with our younger teammates. We laughed, acted crazy, and had fun. We didn't talk about the dark times, we didn't reflect on what had been or could have been. We had accomplished something challenging together, and we wanted to celebrate together. As a team.

The timing could not have been better because our next games were at a tournament in Hawaii. Before the season, we had most looked forward to the trip. Frankly, it was good for us to get out of Waco for a few days.

We won once and lost twice in Hawaii, but the trip was a win for our program.

One day, a group of young kids walked up to us. They were impressed with our heights and the fact that we were college basketball players. They didn't know about any of the other stuff. The look on our guys' faces was priceless as they signed autographs and posed for photos with the kids. In that moment, we were admired for the reasons we all wanted. I realized how much I had missed the awareness that being a D-I player was a special opportunity.

The NCAA reinstated Harvey's eligibility, completing our roster for the tournament. In addition to the nightmare he would create for opposing defenses with his competitiveness and ability to create his own offense, Harvey fit in perfectly. He was downright goofy, in a good way.

Harvey was at the free throw line during one of the tournament games, and Terrance was standing across the free throw lane from me. Harvey pulled his jersey up to wipe sweat from his face, revealing the top of his boxers that appeared to be top-of-the-line Gucci.

"What underwear you wearing, Harv?" Terrance asked him. "Gucci?"

"Naw, man," Harvey said, smiling. "These is Nucci."

Terrance and I were laughing as Harvey shot his free throw while wearing knockoff Gucci boxers. In a no-brainer, "Nucci" became Harvey's nickname for the rest of the season.

The trip also provided us an opportunity to get to know our coaches better on a personal level. Coach Drew continued to impress me. Not that he had been doing anything wrong—I was just too self-absorbed to see it. He genuinely cared about us.

A team dinner set up by tournament officials included dancing contests. We laughed and laughed as Coach Drew and Coach Driscoll attempted to learn a native Hawaiian dance. Coach Drew waved his hands, shook his knees, and had the biggest smile on his face. Our previous staff would not have dared act like that in front of their players. Our staff's tireless work ethic showed even in paradise. Amid all the fun, the coaches were working their phones to recruit players.

My parents and my sister were among the players' families who made the trip. It had become easy to forget that our families had been struggling right along with us. My dad had not missed any of my games, and he had set his schedule to see all the rest too. I was so thankful that Mom, Dad, and Becky had never given up on me.

The most important part of the trip for me came at the Pearl Harbor Memorial.

During our tour, we learned about the more than 2,400 Americans who died in the surprise attack by Japanese aircraft on December 7, 1941. More than 1,100 others were injured. Many were close to my age.

Looking over the side of the memorial, we could still see oil seeping up from the sunken USS Arizona.

The scandal that I had allowed to consume my life suddenly seemed like nothing compared to the tragedy at Pearl Harbor. Thousands had lost their lives, their families' lives were permanently altered, and our country changed forever.

Because of the visit to the memorial, I realized that the troubles we face in life can seem so big and we can feel so alone, as if no one knows what we are going through, but countless others before us have gone through worse times. In my case, I had forgotten that basketball was just a sport. I had dedicated much of my young life to basketball, but it still was *just a sport*.

Every day, people experience loss and heartache with no relief in sight. Of course, our situation at Baylor still mattered. We were having to work through real-life issues. If I ever doubted their reality, all I had to do was remember the nights I tried to drink my troubles away only to wake up to the same problems the following morning.

Being able to zoom out from my life in Hawaii and contemplate what had happened to others on a much larger scale brought a healthy dose of perspective I had been missing. I was grateful to those who gave their lives so we could enjoy our freedom. Because of them, and many others like them fighting for our country around the world, a little boy from Berwick, Pennsylvania, was able to dream and grind to become a college basketball player.

I had many reasons to give thanks for my life.

CONSTANT EFFORT

The good news: we had eleven days off between the Hawaii tournament and our next game. With all five starters averaging close to or over thirty minutes per game, our bodies needed the rest.

The bad news: our next game was against Purdue, the number twenty-one team in the nation.

Legendary coach Gene Keady was in his twenty-fourth season with the Boilermakers, and when I looked over his roster, their height and depth stood out. Purdue boasted eight players at least six-four. We had half that many. Keady also had more players averaging double-figure minutes than we had on scholarship. Included in the Boilermakers' 9–3 record was a ten-point victory over second-ranked Duke.

In a news conference leading up to the game, a reporter asked if I knew how many games I had played. I had no clue. He informed me the Purdue game would be my 101st as a Baylor Bear. Late in the season, barring injury, I could break the record for most games played in program history. I was asked how I felt about nearing the record, and that was a difficult question to answer. Why hadn't previous teammates also approached that record each year? I wasn't sure whether breaking the record would be an achievement to be proud of or if it was the he-stuck-around-the-longest award.

The coaches adjusted our practices to save wear and tear on our bodies. Instead of going head-to-head as much as we had, we worked through five or six stations that allowed us to continue getting good reps and work on skills while minimizing the risk of injuries. The stations work required utilizing all our managers, but at least we had plenty of those.

A rumor started floating that two of our guys were struggling with grades. Nothing against our walk-ons, but I hoped the two weren't scholarship players. With Nucci now in the mix, I finally believed we could put a competitive group together.

Putting on our gear before the pregame walkthrough, I noticed two players not dressing out. Terrance and R.T. were sitting at their lockers with their heads down.

No way, not those two! Anyone else—please!

Coach Drew walked in to address us.

"Okay, obviously, you guys now know that Terrance and R.T. will be sitting out for a while. There's not much for me to say about that, because I know they are beating themselves up." That was true—the pain and shame were evident on their faces. I felt terrible for them.

This was a devastating blow, though, and I could imagine the media having a field day with the news.

"The Baylor men's team just can't seem to do anything right."

Perhaps anticipating the same reaction, the athletic department's news release about Terrance and R.T. mentioned their ineligibility was "not related to the school's internal investigation of its men's basketball program."

We would face the twenty-first-ranked team with only five scholarship players, and Coach Keady could sub in three six-ten players if he wanted. Our first sub would be a walk-on.

Fox Sports Southwest was in Waco to broadcast our first TV appearance of the season. A little over 4,500 fans showed up for our most-attended game to this point. With the TV lights and the bigger-than-usual crowd, the Ferrell Center had a good atmosphere again.

No matter how much effort you give in basketball, bigger is still bigger. It's difficult enough to rebound out of a zone defense, but Purdue also outmatched us physically. Still, we competed well early and were within single digits until back-to-back turnovers led to easy buckets for the Boilers.

Coach pleaded in a timeout, "Take care of the basketball. You have to value each possession."

Our margin of error was too small to throw away possessions.

Purdue ended the first half on a 14–5 run to lead 39–24. If someone had told me that without our leading scorer and best shooter, we would be down only fifteen at the half, I would have been shocked.

Although Purdue was bigger, we were beating ourselves with turn-overs. We could control turnovers, so that gave us a positive feeling for making a second-half comeback.

Will was determined to take advantage of picking up more minutes with Terrance and R.T. out, and he gave us a boost with eight points off the bench. The hit squad made an appearance in the second half to give the starters a rest. Against lesser competition, the subs' fire and energy allowed them to hold their own for several minutes. But the Boilermakers seemed determined to make us pay when the walk-ons were on the floor. And they did. That was the last game in which the hit squad played as a group.

With Purdue leading by twenty-two, Coach looked us straight in the eyes during a timeout. He knew we were tired, and he wasn't upset we were losing so badly. We were giving full effort.

"No matter what you do," he told us, "don't stop playing hard. Keep pushing. Let's get this score back down."

We were likely to lose, but we weren't going to roll over. We gave Purdue all it could handle the rest of the way. A 15–5 run capped by a jumper from Corey brought us within eleven with five minutes left. The crowd's support had increased with each piece of Purdue's lead we chipped away. They had no idea how much hearing their cheers meant to us. We weren't making dynamic plays or playing beautiful basketball, but we were giving our fans authentic effort, and they rewarded us with their approval.

Even in the final minute, we were still competing, and a three-pointer by Nucci with twenty seconds pulled us to within seven. Although we lost 76–65, we had stayed close enough to force the team that had beaten Duke to play hard to the end.

After the final buzzer, I filed in line behind Coach Drew and watched Coach Keady shake his hand and hug him. Keady whispered something to Coach, and I assumed it was a word of encouragement based on how we had played. Coaches throughout the country had to know the challenge Coach Drew and his staff had accepted.

I sat by Coach during the postgame news conference. I was amazed when I looked at the stat sheet on the table in front of us. First, four of our starters—including me—played thirty-six minutes each. That was insane against that level of opponent. Second, we outscored Purdue 41–37 in the second half. How about that!

Losing to Purdue in the manner we did was a confidence booster. With the Big 12 and top-ranked Texas one week away, I couldn't help but be excited at the possibility that we might shock some people.

FACE-TO-FACE WITH MY PROBLEM

Finally, basketball seemed to be in balance again in my life. The big picture was different than I had imagined for my senior year, but we had found a new reason to compete: to accomplish what no one considered possible by being competitive against top teams.

I wish I could say that once at peace with basketball again, the rest of my life neatly fit back into place. But my bad habits remained. My teammates and I worked hard on the court and played hard at night. I turned twenty-two on the day we ended nonconference play with a last-second, one-point loss at home to the University of Texas-Pan American. They beat us on a desperation scoop shot from ten feet that somehow went in.

My one-year relationship with alcohol had transformed my thinking. My sense of right and wrong was skewed. I continued to mute that little voice telling me that I needed something more and that the path I had created wouldn't take me there.

The people who had been unable to understand why I didn't drink or party now were happy I did. Because I was drinking, it was like they could finally accept me. I was no longer standing for something bigger and better around them. Perhaps they didn't feel bad about themselves once I started drinking with them. On the other hand, my friends I had associated with my first two and a half years at Baylor found it hard to identify with me.

Jess called and said she wanted to meet up. We hadn't had a conversation since the Friday after Thanksgiving, when I was at an on-campus party with a lot of people I didn't know. The party had been going on for a few hours, but I had started much earlier. I was out on the porch trying to convince a girl how cool I was when I spotted a familiar car pull up to the curb. My heart stopped. Jess was walking toward the party. I had seen her too late to run inside and out the back door. I sat my beer down behind me, hiding it like people had once done when I entered a party. I needed to act sober so Jess would believe I had stopped by for a few minutes and wasn't staying.

"Hey, there," I said. The words came out slurred. As we made small talk, I wasn't convincing. I tried to act cool and lean against a pole to my left. Except there wasn't a pole there. I crashed to the ground.

When we met up after her call, she broke into tears and told me, "That night I saw you at the party, falling down—I cried on the way home."

I felt ashamed, briefly. Jess continued to live righteously, and everything about her life reflected that. She might have said the same about me before I started partying.

Then I justified my behaviors by lying to myself.

She doesn't understand. Her team is on its way to the NCAA Tournament. She hasn't gone through what I have. Who could blame me for trying to have a little fun?

Basketball was fine now; it no longer was my problem.

I was my problem.

17

ERASING THE ZERO

The bus ride to Austin was almost two hours. I had plenty of time to think about our first conference opponent, the Texas Longhorns.

Texas was ranked eighteenth coming off its Final Four appearance the year before, and the Frank Erwin Center was among the toughest arenas we played in. With Terrance and R.T. ineligible, I was the only senior who would dress out. Texas had five seniors who I had played against since we were freshmen.

This would be my eighth game against the Longhorns, and more than any of the younger players, I understood this game was bigger than just our two teams. Baylor and Texas had met 216 times since 1905— our most games against any opponent. It would require a thorough search to find fans more arrogant than Texas fans. Admittedly, they had a right to be. Not only had we lost all seven of my games against Texas, but we had lost to them by fewer than ten points only twice.

Texas was straight-up physical with big, strong guys—and lots of them. Fortunately, point guard T.J. Ford had opted to leave after the previous season to enter the NBA. I didn't want to think about chasing him around for forty minutes.

Nine guys suited up. In addition to us being without Terrance and R.T., Joe did not make the trip because of a family emergency.

Most of those nine had not played in front of a crowd the size of the 8,700 in the Erwin Center. Before the opening tip, I wanted to acknowledge each of the other eight with a hug, hand slap, or pat on the back. I looked each in the eye to make sure we were ready.

UT won the tip, and we opened with a solid defensive possession in our zone. We forced the Longhorns to keep the ball on the perimeter and out of the hands of their larger inside players. Royal Ivy let fly a deep three that was wide right, and Carl ran down the rebound. Our bench and small number of fans stood and applauded holding off the Longhorns' first charge.

Texas coach Rick Barnes' strategy quickly became evident: he wanted to wear us down on the offensive end. UT's defense hounded us, forcing our idiot motion offense into bad shots and turnovers. On the inbounds pass following the Longhorns' first free throws, they surprised us with a 1-2-2 three-quarter trap. I crossed half-court, and two defenders swarmed me and ripped the ball out of my hands to set up a UT bucket. Our ensuing possession ended with another turnover.

We didn't make a field goal for almost four and a half minutes, when we were already behind 10–1. Fittingly for how hard Texas was making us work, the points came when Nucci made a shot while falling to the floor. We followed that possession with a dunk with authority by Tommy off an offensive rebound. We were showing signs of recovering from the poor start.

Then, five minutes into the game, UT subbed in three fresh players. Robbie was our first sub, coming in for Tommy. Texas's six-eight center James Thomas grinned when he saw his new matchup.

My first points came on a tough drive, cutting our deficit to 24–19 with less than seven minutes until halftime. No one would have expected us to be this close. We still were down five a couple of minutes later when one of our players slammed Brad Buckman, forcing him to make free throws rather than scoring an easy basket. I liked that! I wanted us to make Texas earn their points too.

During the free throws, I told Corey, "Take number 10."

"What, you don't know my name now?" the Texas player asked.

It was Kenny Taylor. I hadn't seen him since the basement meeting when Coach Bliss told us he was stepping down. Kenny was the first of the former teammates I had reunited with, and I wanted to hug him and ask how he was doing. But he was wearing the enemy's burnt orange and white now. I settled for giving him a little smile.

No surprise, Texas was too deep and too good for us. The Longhorns ended the first half on a 15–6 run, started the second with a 12–2 run, and cruised to a 79–57 victory. We never backed down, though, and I liked our effort throughout.

I played all but one minute and was worn out when the final buzzer sounded. During the game, UT fans had reminded me why I disliked them so much. As if I needed a reminder. But on our way off the floor, I heard applause. I turned toward the other end, expecting to see the Texas players walking off the court. But no Longhorns were in sight.

I looked into the seats to see several hundred UT fans, decked out in burnt orange, looking in our direction and clapping. I was stunned. I had never witnessed anything like this in sports, and I sure wouldn't have expected it to occur at UT. Our effort had earned their respect. I wondered if our younger guys could grasp how significant that moment was. Despite the twenty-two-point margin, we had traveled to Austin and found our version of success.

CLOSE ISN'T GOOD ENOUGH

I had not read many positive articles involving our program over the past seven months, but I read great news the day before our next game, against Texas Tech.

Terrance and R.T.'s eligibility had been reinstated. The university had requested a waiver from the NCAA on the players' behalf. Michael Rogers, Baylor's faculty representative to the Big 12 Conference and the NCAA, was quoted as saying, "While this waiver decision by the NCAA is based on the merits, it is full of grace and understanding. It was granted because of the totality of circumstances and events of the past six months, which have been unique and unimaginable." Finally, someone seemed to understand our situation. And, boy, did we need Terrance and R.T.—probably more than any program needed two players.

Texas Tech came into Waco ranked number twenty-two—one of nine Big 12 games we would play against a ranked opponent. Our two other seniors were back, and I enjoyed the optimism and energy in our program. I had anticipated starting the Big 12 schedule would stamp out the last bit of life we had, but I could not deny the influence Coach Drew and his staff held over our team. Somehow, they had made good on their promise to instill hope in our locker room.

Now, nothing could derail our mission of accomplishing the unexpected. When Joe decided to step away from the team, we didn't skip a beat. It wasn't easy being a walk-on, and it had to be extra challenging to be a walk-on with the leftovers.

The Big 12 had a list of amazing coaches I respected—Rick Barnes at Texas, Eddie Sutton at Oklahoma State, Roy Williams and then Bill Self at Kansas. But to me, none of them compared to

Tech's Bobby Knight. Chills ran down my spine during games hearing "The General" barking at one of his players as I ran past his sideline. Knowing that Coach Bliss had been Coach Knight's first assistant coach and having enjoyed playing for Bliss, I would have loved playing in Coach Knight's program. Some would question that based on Knight's well-known outbursts. But I considered him disciplined, organized, and a master teacher, and I thrived in that type of environment. Plus, I believed he would have appreciated my approach to the game.

Coach Drew went with a seven-man rotation, and Coach Knight played his starters heavy minutes too. Best against best, we locked up in a back-and-forth game. With 9:47 left in the game, R.T.'s follow put us up 48–47. We weren't just hanging around and keeping it close—we were positioned to win. During a timeout, as we were walking toward our huddle, our fans were going crazy. This was more like how I had envisioned my senior year, as a vital part of a team capable of beating the best in the country.

Terrance was sensational, scoring twenty points and reminding us what his presence meant to our team. With less than six minutes to go and a chance to take the lead, Tommy missed a layup that seemed to do everything but go through the basket. Tech outscored us 20–6 the rest of the way for a 75–66 victory, dropping our record to 5–10 overall and 0–2 in conference. The crowd of almost 8,000 gave us a standing ovation. Although we weren't pursuing moral victories—I don't believe in them—the ovation added to the healing process from the boos after the UTSA game a month earlier.

Coach Drew's postgame speech was familiar—he was proud of our persistent effort. But then he added, "Are you okay with just being close, or do you really want to beat some of these guys?"

We wanted to win. We needed to win. And our coach expected us to win.

My young teammates did not need long to get smacked in the face by the difficulty of playing in our conference. Each night, we had to be sharp and fight our butts off just to compete. But we legitimately believed that on any given night, with constant effort and a solid performance, we had the ability to upset anyone. On the flip side, anything less and any game could get out of hand in a hurry.

I dreaded the trip to play Nebraska. Lincoln seemed like it was in the middle of nowhere, the weather was cold, and the Cornhuskers' arena was always packed with anti-Baylor fans. On the road, we were all we had. In Lincoln, Terrance came up with an appropriate saying for breaking out of our huddles: "We all we got!"

We missed our first thirteen shots in falling behind 12–1. Nebraska fans laughed at us. I couldn't blame them. I made our first field goal on a three-pointer, and that didn't occur until 7:10 remained in the first half. Our shooting got better—how could it not?—but the night didn't. Corey landed awkwardly after a missed dunk and missed the rest of the game.

Honestly, our effort was good at Nebraska; we just played poorly. The 76–47 loss demonstrated what would happen in the Big 12 if we had an off night.

When losses start mounting up—we had lost five in a row—staying positive is difficult. Our coaching staff made it almost impossible to feel sorry for ourselves. Their energy was contagious. The previous coaching staff used verbal and sometimes physical threats in rough stretches like this one. Coach Drew's staff created an atmosphere that made us want to show up to practice after a loss.

And back to work we went the next day. Iowa State (11–3, 2–1) would be in Waco in two days.

NO "REFLECTING BACK"

"We all we got!" With that said—and Corey back after leaving the Nebraska game—we headed out of the locker room.

It turned out that we weren't all we had on this night. Almost 6,000 fans were inside the arena. We'd had larger crowds this season, but I couldn't remember one that was louder. The Ferrell Center sounded sold out.

The fans came for excitement and entertainment, and our team and Iowa State started the game providing neither. Unless a blooper reel counts as entertainment.

Missed shots. Turnovers. Wasted possessions. Probably the only two highlights in the first half were electrifying dunks by Tommy. But he racked up three fouls in three minutes and had to head to the bench. We had watched this movie before: our small team competes for a stretch until fatigue or foul trouble set in.

With six minutes remaining in the first half, Iowa State led 10–8. Eighteen total points in fourteen minutes! I hoped our fans weren't making plans to leave at halftime.

Both teams got hot—relatively speaking—to end the half, and we took a 21–20 lead into the locker room. We had not scored twenty-one points in a first half and still led since the 1994–95 season.

The second half looked like an actual Division I game. We led most of the half and were ahead 54–49 with 2:36 to play. We had to finish this, and our fans—who had graciously stuck around after the first half—wanted a win as desperately as us.

Heart and emotion were two of Nucci's biggest strengths, but they worked against him when he didn't like a ref's call and wouldn't let it go. The ref whistled him for a technical foul, giving Iowa State two free throws and the ball. The Cyclones made both free throws and scored from underneath the basket on the ensuing possession. Just like that, our lead was down to one.

Terrance made a jumper to push our lead to three. Iowa State called a timeout, and Coach Drew must have seen fear on our faces as we came to the sideline. I know I was feeling it, worried that we were letting another victory get away from us.

"You can do this!" Coach snapped. "You deserve this! Go make it happen!"

R.T. made two free throws out of the timeout, and Iowa State answered with a bucket. I made one of two free throws, and the Cyclones hit another jumper on their end. Our lead was 59–57 with twenty-eight seconds left.

We could have put the game away, but we missed two of four free throws in the closing half-minute, and Iowa State scored again with three seconds left. We led 61–59. R.T. grabbed a crucial loose ball and flipped it to Carl, who was fouled with one second remaining. With a two-point lead, we should have felt pretty good about our chances. But we had too much history with things not going our way to relax. We needed Carl to make both free throws.

Our freshman point guard looked timid walking to the line. I flashed back to the Louisiana Monroe game, when Carl could have iced the game in regulation but missed a second free throw. ULM hit a three to tie, and we needed double overtime to eke out the win. I love that basketball is a game of redemption. As players, we have to stay prepared because that chance at redemption often comes unannounced.

Carl made both free throws, and the crowd was at a louder-than-sold-out level as an Iowa State player heaved the ball downcourt with no opportunity to tie the score. The buzzer sounded, and I threw my fist into the air and pointed to our student section. I loved being able to enjoy this moment with them.

As one large group, we stood with our right hands in the air—"Sic 'Em" proudly on display—and sang "That Good Old Baylor Line."

We had just won a Big 12 game, accomplishing what no one in the country thought we could. In the locker room, we were yelling and jumping into each other's arms. A few players cried. A whole variety of emotions was on display at once. Our record was 6–11, and we were celebrating like we had won a championship. Every game for us *was* a championship.

Coach Drew strolled in like a conquering hero and headed straight to the whiteboard. To motivate us before conference play started, he had written the number of Big 12 games we were predicted to win. He grabbed the marker, erased the zero, and emphatically replaced it with a "1." We responded with whoops and hollers. With little to play for, proving people wrong had become a powerful motivator. And we did.

After we calmed down, Coach Drew proclaimed, "Now no one will ask us if we will win a Big 12 game!"

In the postgame media interview, I said, "We're happy and thankful that our fans stuck with us through the hard times. We won this for the fans."

The next question started with, "Matt, reflecting back over the summer…"

I wanted to grab the reporter and shake him. The media seemed to be the only ones not moving on from the summer. Even after we had just accomplished what the media considered unthinkable, they seemed focused on what we had lost and what could have been.

I was proud to be a part of this team and tired of politely answering idiotic questions "correctly" instead of making my true thoughts known. I told Heath after the media session, "I am done 'reflecting back' and I will refuse to answer questions like that in the future."

A few days later, Heath asked me to go to our smaller media room to answer a few questions. I looked forward to touting what we had achieved amid adversity. A reporter asked me to "reflect back." I stared at her blankly. My smile probably looked pretty creepy as I said, "When

I was little, before every game, my mother made peanut butter pancakes. But my mother can't come on the road with me. So, on the road, I take my own peanut butter and make my own peanut butter pancakes. It's a ritual that I will not let go of." The reporter's confused look was priceless. I smiled as I wondered what I had caused to happen inside her brain.

This season would no longer be about the past. We had proved that playing against the leftovers was not a rollover game. If opponents didn't prepare for us, we just might mess up their postseason plans.

18

VALIDATION FOR ALL

I was out of breath and wanted to stick my head in the visiting locker room's water cooler. We were tied at halftime with number nineteen Texas Tech, and I was gassed. I wasn't the only one feeling the effects of playing at least thirty-five minutes in most games.

Our two losses since the Iowa State win had made things worse.

I had never been forced to work as hard just to get open as I had against Oklahoma's tenacious defense. Then two days later, we played in Boulder, Colorado. I don't know the math on the effects of altitude, but playing thirty-seven minutes at 5,400 feet was not close to playing thirty-seven minutes in Waco, which is just 470 feet above sea level. Plus, Corey fractured his right hand in the Colorado game, dropping us back to six scholarship players.

I couldn't deny that the most significant issue affecting my conditioning was my partying and poor eating habits. I know I would have played better had I stopped drinking and stuck to a healthier diet. But unlike some of my teammates, my body wasn't built for heavy minutes to begin with. I thought I would be most productive at twenty to twenty-five minutes per game. But, shoot, most nights, I was playing close to twenty minutes in the *first half.*

Our senior trio had played efficiently in the first half at Tech. Athletes in various sports often talk about the game slowing down for them. The games can't actually slow down, of course, but when an athlete can process information at the same pace as the game, he or she feels like the game is slower. For the first time this season, I had reached that state. I was comfortable in my role, and my play reflected my comfort.

Coach Knight was furious with his players late in the first half. After we had run off a 20–6 spurt, he upped the game's tempo. Our same ol' problem resurfaced, and fatigue began to wear away at us. Late in the second half, a shooting foul was called. I slumped over for the free throws, grabbing at my shorts, trying to quickly locate some air. I felt a hand rest on my back, followed by, "You a little tired?"

Without looking, I replied, "More than a little."

Smiling, I turned to see the question had come from one of the referees. Over my Baylor career, I had treated refs with respect. I had been the first to chase down loose balls and hand them to the refs, and I tried to be a good player with whom they could communicate. As a result, I had developed good relationships with many of the Big 12 officials. Most called me by my first name. Little exchanges like the one with that ref brought a personal element to the games that enriched my D-I experience.

Once our legs had left us, as they had in this game, we were prone to turnovers, missed shots, and failing to block out on rebounds. That led to runs by our opponents from which we could not recover. Against Tech, the run that did us in was the Red Raiders' 21–8 advantage over the first seven minutes of the second half. We lost 83–63.

I enjoyed shaking opposing coaches' hands after games. While Roy Williams was still coaching at Kansas, he pulled me in close and told me, "You guys outworked us today." Even though we had lost, Coach Williams' comment meant a lot to me.

Coach Knight was different than most coaches we played against. After our first game against Tech my sophomore year, I was eager to greet him. But after he shook Coach Bliss's hand, he bolted for the door.

Because this was my last game against Tech, I made a beeline for him at midcourt. I called out, "Coach Knight!" and approached him with my hand out.

"The General" was six-five, and his intimidating presence made it feel like he towered over me. He caught me off-guard by placing an arm around me and calling me by name. Coach Knight knew my name!

"Matt, I have always appreciated you," he told me. "I want you to know that if I had been here when you came out of high school, I would have recruited you hard."

I wasn't sure if my heart was beating.

"Thank you, Coach," I managed to say before he resumed his quick exit.

For the type of player I was, Coach Knight's compliment was monumental. Most of the time, I felt like my effort and value went unnoticed, especially by opposing teams. He probably had no idea how rewarding it was for someone of his stature to not only acknowledge my abilities but say that he would have wanted me on his team. Obviously, I still have a detailed memory of the moment.

Coach Drew and our coaching staff were receiving big-time respect around the league and in the media. Coach Drew was often mentioned as a potential winner of the Big 12 Coach of the Year award even though we had one conference victory. How realistic the possibility was, I had no idea. But he would have deserved it. He was showing the nation that coaching was about more than wins and losses. Coaching also could be about overcoming crushing odds and helping young people discover what they are capable of achieving. His motivating style prevented players from quitting on themselves.

Baylor basketball was expected to be bad for a long time because of the scandal and punishments, but twenty games into Coach Drew's first season, he had changed the perception of our program. He had caused us to rally around the realization that we were establishing the foundation for the Baylor teams to come.

SIGN OF MATURITY

Coach Drew had preached to us that opportunities could become available to each of us as our program rebuilt. The key to taking advantage of those opportunities, he told us, was to maintain the right mindset.

Indeed, many of us were finding individual successes on this side of the mess.

Terrance and Harvey were enjoying monster seasons. Terrance was the Big 12's second-leading scorer at 17.2 points per game. What a transformation from his junior season, when he couldn't find his way off the bench. Nucci was chipping in 15.5 points a game along with six rebounds. R.T. was a game or two from moving into ninth place at Baylor for three-pointers made in a career. I was close to becoming seventh in assists, fourth in games played, seventh in steals, and eighth in total minutes played.

Tommy also was closing in on the Baylor top-ten list—for most games fouled out. We roasted Tommy over that stat!

From my observation, consistency was the most important trait in successful basketball players. I had watched numerous more-talented players fizzle out. I shook my head thinking about most of them because all they had to do to succeed was keep their priorities right. For me, I needed to prioritize consistency in high effort.

Even this season, with all its adversity, merely sticking around—as I had always found a way to do—was producing a different kind of success for our team. My teammates and I kept showing up. "Showing up" doesn't sound extraordinary in a society that celebrates the winners. But the fact that we were even here, combined with our effort, was forcing Baylor basketball into conversations around the league and, to a degree, around the country. And they were talking about us for the right reasons—the very reasons I had come to Baylor.

Not that showing up and giving effort were easy. The volume of minutes the starters were logging was draining us. My pregame routine included pain medication downed by an energy drink. Each player was nursing his own aches and pains. We were scrappy and tough, but we also were human with limits on how much our bodies could take. The coaches were fantastic about looking out for our health. They monitored us during practices and scaled back when we were reaching our edge—because they cared about us. I owed them an apology for my hesitancy toward them at the beginning of the season. I believed the best way to express my regrets was to allow my effort to speak for me.

No matter how much we ached and how tired we were, there was nothing like an opportunity to win a game to reinvigorate us.

Despite riding a three-game losing skid, we still believed we possessed the capability of beating any Big 12 opponent. But to look at the schedule and see what we considered a *very* winnable game? We finally had one of those, with the only team below us in the conference standings coming to the Ferrell Center: the last-place Texas A&M Aggies, who were 7–11 overall and 0–7 in league play.

Both universities were situated near the Brazos River, about ninety miles apart. The schools' annual football games were billed as "The Battle of the Brazos." This game was the 188th meeting in our basketball rivalry, which began during the 1914–15 season when the Aggies held off the Bears by a yawn-inducing score of 39–14. Three seasons later, the Aggies defeated us 19–6. That game had to be fun to watch!

This year's Aggies were certainly higher-scoring, with the offense led by sophomore guard/forward Antoine Wright, who went on to become a first-round pick in the NBA draft. We knew we had to prevent Wright from going off, but even Coach Drew had let us know this was a "very winnable" game.

Leading the team out of the tunnel to play A&M felt like I was in my freshman year again and number six Kansas was in town. The 7,000 fans were rocking the place in anticipation of the opening tip. Some of them were Aggies, but they were easy to spot. All we had to do was look for anyone wearing overalls and a straw hat—that was definitely an Aggie. I loved beating the Aggies just because of their fans' never-ceasing chants and swaying.

Our team was flying from the start. We did a great job accounting for A&M's shooters, and we controlled the game's pace to our favor. With us leading by one in the closing seconds of the first half, R.T. swung the ball to me, and I nailed a three that sent us to halftime leading 30–26. The shot had our fans going insane as we sprinted toward the locker room. I momentarily wanted to stop and soak in the moment. I had missed feeling a part of something special, and that was back. In some ways, this feeling was more special than any in my previous three years.

Our strong first half had us confident in the locker room. But we weren't overconfident. For one, if there was one team that could never afford to be overconfident, we were the unanimous choice to be that team. Second, the Aggies disliked us as much as we disliked them. We were going to get everything they could give us in the second half.

We started the half with a 13–4 run. Our lead soon grew to fifteen points—our largest lead in a game since the start of Big 12 play. Our lead was still at fifteen after Harvey smashed a nasty dunk for a 56–41 advantage with 6:30 to play. Little did we know that would be our last field goal of the game.

The Aggies twice fought back to within four points of us. Fortunately, we were making our free throws. We scored our final sixteen points at the line, including making twelve of our sixteen attempts in the final two minutes, and won 72–64. Nucci and I both scored twenty points. I made eleven of thirteen free throws in setting my career high for points. Equally satisfying was seeing how much our young players had matured. Going six and a half minutes without scoring from the field could have caused them to panic because, as Coach Drew told the media, we hadn't played many games where we led by double digits with five minutes to go. "We've got to work on that," he joked.

We waited with anticipation for Coach to come into our locker room because we knew the first thing he would do. Sure enough, he marched directly to the board, erased the "1" that had sat there for two weeks, and wrote a beautiful "2."

Beating A&M was about more than earning a second Big 12 victory. It validated that every player had made the right choice to stay.

Including me.

19

THE BIG 12 MONSTER

Halfway through the conference schedule, we had defeated two Big 12 teams. On the one hand, we had already far exceeded expectations. But on the other, the coaches were keeping us upbeat and always focused on our next opponent.

This team had more energy and life than any on which I had played. Terrance and I were on-court leaders who off the court accepted any dare presented to us. Nucci, Carl, Tommy, R.T., and Corey contributed their unique characteristics to the fun we had with each other. I laughed so much every day that I felt like I had worked on my abs in the weight room.

On my way to class, my phone rang. It was nice to no longer dread seeing who was calling me. This time, it was my mom.

"Hey, what's up?"

"Matt, I have to tell you what happened at work." Mom sounded excited. "Do you have a minute?"

"Sure, Mom."

"Yesterday, a guy came into the pharmacy, and he was wearing a Baylor shirt. When he got close to me, I said, 'Do you go to Baylor?' He says, 'Yeah. It's been a crazy year for us.' So I said, 'My son plays basketball there. His name is Matt.' Then he lights up and says, 'Matt Sayman?' I told him yes, and he just went on and on about you and how proud he was of your effort and that you stayed. I was so excited that I wanted to call you last night, but I got home too late. So this is the first chance I had to call!"

"Thanks, Mom. I needed that."

"I'm so proud of you," she said. "I hope you know that."

"I do, Mom. Thanks."

After all the negativity and all the times it felt as though everyone was against us, Mom's call meant a lot. I still needed to hear that people—especially from our student body and our community—respected what we were doing.

As I continued to walk, I teared up thinking about how much my mom had gone through. She had watched her son's dream shatter. She had heard her son blamed for things he didn't do. She even heard the UNT fans call me a murderer. She deserved to hear something good from that guy in the pharmacy as much as I did.

When I had started shifting away from thinking about how much people owed me, I became aware of how much I owed the people around me.

I don't know how much my parents knew about my lifestyle, but let's be honest, parents always know something! They still were proud of me. They still loved me. They had given me everything they could throughout my life, and I wanted to show them a return on their investment by finishing my college career strong. I owed them that.

I also owed the team my best effort over our final eight games together. My teammates had stood with me when I was "me first, them second." Over the final month of the season, I needed to focus, play hard, and do everything I could to ensure that regardless of whether we won another game, people would know that Baylor basketball stood for effort.

The next three games were a tough stretch even by Big 12 standards: at home against Texas and road games at Oklahoma State and Kansas. All three were ranked nationally.

The Texas game marked the first return to our campus of one of the big three who left. The media were asking questions about Kenny coming back to Waco. I understood it was a good story. But, personally, I wanted to focus on being competitive against Texas, which had moved up to number eleven in the country since our first meeting.

"I respect Kenny for the decision he made," I said. "I hope that everyone treats him the right way."

I liked Kenny, and I had no issue with his reason for leaving. But I knew our fans would think differently. Sure enough, each time Kenny touched the ball, the entire crowd of 6,000 booed and chanted "Traitor." After Kenny missed his first three-point shot, the crowd roared in delight. I was sure Kenny expected that type of greeting, and he delivered the perfect response: eighteen points, all on six three-pointers. He made four threes in the first half, as Texas jumped out to a 36–19 lead at halftime.

Eleven UT players played double-digit minutes, and no one played more than twenty-one. Without Corey, four of us played at least thirty-one minutes. I was wiped out from guarding Royal Ivy hard for five minutes only to see a fresh Brandon Mouton sub in for him.

Outmatched, we lost 84–58. As I hugged Kenny after the game, I wished he was still on my side.

Four days later, we were in Stillwater to play tenth-ranked Oklahoma State and, for the first time, John Lucas. There was no better arena in the country than Gallagher-Iba Arena because the seating seemed like it went straight up. With a capacity over 13,000, having that many fans close to the court made the place deafening. At various times in its long history, OSU's arena had been known as "The Madison Square Garden of the Plains" and "The Rowdiest Arena in the Country."

I missed Kenny. John was a different story. There were no smiles from either of us the first time we saw each other. I wanted to win this game, and I wanted to show John that he shouldn't have taken my job when he came to Baylor.

So much for that idea.

Under Coach Sutton, John had blossomed into one of the nation's top point guards. Not only was he playing unbelievably, but his surrounding cast—including future pros Tony Allen and the Graham twins, Joey and Stephen—was too much for the six of us. I accounted for 36 percent of our first-half points—and I scored five. We were beaten by halftime, trailing 43–14.

The 91–58 loss butt-whipping was our worst yet. Coach Drew couldn't say much afterward except that we didn't have a lot of time to feel sorry for ourselves and had to get on the bus. Next stop: Lawrence, Kansas, and the number twenty-one Kansas Jayhawks. Gotta love the Big 12!

A MATTER OF PERSPECTIVE

We arrived in Lawrence the night before the game, and even for a game against the leftovers, students were camping out next to Allen Fieldhouse for tickets. With all the history Allen Fieldhouse contained, walking in was intimidating. Inside, I could sense pride in the program. During our practice, I noticed Kansas had sweet Wilson-brand basketballs branded with their Jayhawk logo. The balls weren't available for sale, so only people inside the program could own one.

Despite their ranking, the Jayhawks were coming off their first back-to-back losses of at least nineteen points since 1919. Coach Self would have his players prepared to make a statement against us.

With a game against an opponent in that spot the next day, most teams would likely get to sleep early. Not our team. We found ways to keep the season interesting.

Will texted me that night at the hotel to come to his and Ryan's room. I figured they had made up some new game they wanted to show me. I walked into their room, and they were fully dressed in practice gear. They had…ahem, *found* some souvenirs in the form of the Jayhawk-branded basketballs. The balls were awesome. We spent the next hour snapping player pictures and action shots in their room. (I'm hoping the statute of limitations has expired; I'm not sure what happened to my souvenir!)

Much to the dismay of the 16,300 fans face-painted in Kansas' crimson and blue, we were down only two with under thirteen minutes remaining in the game. Harvey and R.T. were highly efficient in scoring, and we were limiting Kansas to tough shots around the perimeter. We had trailed by five at halftime only because the Jayhawks scored five unanswered points to end the half, and I hadn't noticed any significant adjustments on Kansas's part in the second half. But they were subbing guys in and out, keeping fresh players on the court.

One downside to our zone defense was that if a team started hitting three-pointers, we would have to spread out to adjust, creating space on the inside. J.R. Giddens made a couple of long-range bombs that stretched KU's lead to ten inside the ten-minute mark. Neither Terrance nor I had had a meaningful break—I played thirty-nine minutes, he played thirty-eight—so it was the same story of our lack of depth leading to fatigue.

We didn't have enough in the tank to put together a run against the Jayhawks' fresh players. With just under seven minutes left, we were down thirteen when Carl fouled a player going up for a shot. Those of us on the floor briefly huddled, out of breath. When Carl strolled into the huddle, in a nonchalant tone like he was telling us he ate a sandwich that day, he informed us that he had fouled out. We broke out in laughter. That's what made being a part of this team special. In Allen Fieldhouse, down thirteen and worn out, the five of us were laughing in the middle of the court.

Over the previous ten games, I had intentionally communicated more on the court to my teammates. The coaching staff began calling me "Coach Sayman." At first, I considered it a joke between the coaches, but over time, I noticed they respected my opinions. With five minutes left, Kansas's lead was getting close to twenty points. It was frustrating knowing that we were going toe-to-toe with the Jayhawks in their place until our lack of depth caught up with us. Again.

One of our operations directors on the sideline—not an assistant coach—was yelling at the ref over some call or non-call he didn't like. The ref turned to yell at the bench to cut out the griping. I turned to our coaches and yelled at them to stop our guy from chirping. He probably was frustrated like the rest of us, but our players didn't need to hear that mess coming from our sideline. We certainly didn't need a technical foul or the refs to get upset with us because of someone who wasn't playing or coaching. By yelling toward our coach, I knew I had done something players rarely get away with. But I believed it was my job to represent our guys on the court at that moment. I never heard a word from the guy on the bench again. I guess the coaches knew I was correct.

We lost 74–54. Anyone who watched the game knew the final margin did not represent how competitive the game was. Coach Self and the Kansas program were first class. He shook my hand and said,

"You guys played really hard." For most of my career, anything but winning was not enough. But Coach Self's words made me feel proud of our team.

I held a ton of respect for Kansas forward Wayne Simien as a competitor. When I heard what he told the media about us after the game, his words further validated what we were doing. "I have a lot of respect for those guys," he said. "They played us really hard and smart. We had a lot of trouble with that zone all the way through the first half."

I left Allen Fieldhouse sad that I would never play there again. OSU had the best arena, but Allen Fieldhouse was the most special place to play. I would have preferred saying goodbye with a victory, but the way we left has made for wonderful memories.

The bus ride to the airport demonstrated the perspective Coach Drew instilled in us. Our number one priority was seeing who could create the best impression of Carl telling us he had fouled out.

THAT FAMILIAR STING

Coming off the three losses against ranked teams, we weren't catching much of a break with a game against Missouri. Three seniors—Ricky Paulding, Arthur Johnson, and Travon Bryant—gave the Tigers a trio with four years of solid experience together. With a 6–5 conference record, the Tigers were a middle-of-the-pack team separated from the elite teams by only several possessions per game. They had started the season with legitimate NCAA Tournament aspirations, and with a 12–10 record, they could not afford to lose many more games. A loss to us could have been devastating for their postseason chances.

Because of Missouri's failure to meet expectations, Coach Quin Snyder's job was in jeopardy when his team came to our place. Before the game, he was in shorts, making a show of working out his team and sweating along with them. I had witnessed coaches try a lot of things to win games. Snyder seemed to want everyone in the Ferrell Center to know he was trying anything he could to save his job. Coach Driscoll didn't hide his disapproval of Coach Snyder's performance from us.

When I was in eighth grade, Coach Snyder was my outdoor instruction coach at a Duke basketball camp. I had wanted to talk to him in previous seasons, but I did not feel secure enough to start a conversation. Now, I walked over to him during warm-ups and sat next to him. He looked a little surprised.

"Coach Snyder, I know you don't remember this," I told him, "but you were my outdoor instruction coach at a Duke basketball camp when I was in the eighth grade. At the time, you gave me some very good advice."

He laughed. "Really? What advice was that?"

"You told us that when it came to finding a wife, we shouldn't marry the pretty girls, but instead marry the fat girls because they will never leave you, and they cook really good food."

Coach Snyder burst out laughing.

"Oh, Matt. Those were the good ole days."

I laughed with him, and we made some small talk before shaking hands and going our separate ways.

We had our seventh scholarship player back, with Corey returning after missing six games because of the hand fracture. We led by as many as seven points in the first half, but Missouri took the lead four minutes before intermission. Down one point at halftime, 33–32, our confidence was soaring, and that carried over into the second half. Less than three minutes in, we were up by five again. The home crowd was sensing another upset.

Missouri worked its way to a five-point lead, and then the experience in tight games we had accumulated showed as we started chipping away at our deficit. There was a loose ball on Missouri's end, and as it bounced toward the corner, Tommy flew in and saved it while getting undercut. I quickly secured the ball and was fouled. I sank both free throws and with 4:30 left, we were tied at 61.

During a timeout, we sprinted to our bench. The usual guys were playing their usual minutes. We were so locked in on the possibility of winning that, although we should have been tired, we weren't.

I later watched a recording of the ESPN telecast, and during one of the timeouts, the two announcers talked about their expectations before observing our pregame practice. Teams with a record like ours often give up on the season. But the commentators described their surprise at how much fun we were having together. Music was blaring during practice, and Coach Drew was walking around full of energy and laughing. The commentators said without knowing the circumstances, they would have assumed we were a winning team.

We were down three during a timeout with forty-nine seconds left, and Coach wanted us to foul to force Missouri to make free throws. On the inbounds play, Missouri threw the ball to half-court and swung it quickly to Paulding. Carl and I sprinted to trap Paulding, and a ref called a travel. Carl and I both turned down threes on our possession, and we worked the ball inside to Harvey for a layup that brought us to within one with twenty-nine seconds to play.

Coach Drew called timeout and instructed us to foul immediately. It took longer than we wanted, but we fouled Paulding with eighteen seconds left.

I took my place alongside the free throw lane. I was facing the Tigers' bench, and when I looked in that direction, all their players had their arms interlocked with each other like teams often did late in a big, tension-filled game. Missouri was worried about losing to us.

Paulding connected on both free throws, and we were down three again. Coach Drew took his last timeout to set up a play.

I brought the ball up the floor. We set screens for R.T. and Terrance, hoping Missouri's defense wouldn't communicate on the screens and leave one of them open. But Missouri switched well on the screens and nothing opened. The ball came back to me twenty-four feet from the basket and with six seconds on the clock. In those situations, you have to make a quick decision and stick with it. I caught the ball in rhythm and launched a long, off-balance three for the tie. The shot felt good leaving my hand, but it started drifting right on its way to the basket. The ball caromed off the rim and to a Missouri player.

We had to foul Paulding again to stop the clock with two seconds remaining. I bent over and grabbed my shoes in frustration.

We lost 70–66. Yet again, we had come close without being able to finish. Obviously, we could be proud of our effort and performance. Just being competitive required a lot from us. But we were placing ourselves in situations where we could win—and, we believed, should win. The sting I felt was the same as I had experienced in the playoffs my senior year at The Colony. As a freshman in our NIT loss. The previous year in the Big 12 tournament loss to Texas Tech.

I desperately wanted that shot back. I wanted one more chance to help our team win. Then, unexpectedly, I felt a slight grin on my face.

The leftovers were not the Big 12's doormat. Our opponents could not look at us a throwaway game. They had better be prepared to play us.

HOW "SWEEP" IT IS

We had an unchecked box I wanted to take care of: win a road game. We had won a neutral-court game against Northern Illinois in the Hawaii tournament, but we had yet to walk into an opponent's arena and hand them a loss.

One team was worse off than us in the Big 12. Texas A&M still had not won a conference game. Oh-for-12. Nobody was calling our game in College Station a "very winnable" game, but on the bus ride, we all knew we could win this game on the road.

With 5,000 Aggies fans swaying and chanting, we forced A&M into our style of game—ugly and scrappy. The game was hard-fought and close throughout. Terrance tied the score on a jumper with fourteen seconds left. But then he made the mistake of fouling Antoine Wright, A&M's leading scorer, with three seconds remaining.

I dropped my head. Another close game we let get away.

Inexplicably, Wright missed both free throws, and we went into overtime.

We dominated overtime, opening the extra five minutes by scoring ten of the first twelve points. At one point, the five of us on the floor circled up. Terrance and I were coming up on forty minutes played at that point.

Terrance said three words: "We got this."

And we did. I scored eight of my fifteen points during overtime, and we won 67–61 to sweep our two games with the Aggies and send their fans home upset. The fans apparently weren't the only ones upset because A&M fired its head coach, Melvin Watkins, the next day. I guess the final straw was losing to us a second time.

Coach Driscoll and Coach Tang walked off the court with their arms around me. They had to feel that each win by our team, perhaps even each close game, pushed our program one more step down the road to becoming the contender they envisioned. Inside the locker room, we were shaking soda cans and spraying them on each other. Terrance grabbed a marker and triumphantly wrote a big "3" and circled it on the board. We all cheered. This team—players and coaches—was more of a family than any group I had been a part of.

Big 12 frontrunner Oklahoma State and John Lucas came to Waco four days later, exactly two weeks after smacking us in the face by thirty-three points. The Cowboys had climbed to number six in the nation. ESPN+ was broadcasting the game, and I didn't expect many people to tune in for this matchup.

The ones who decided not to watch missed out.

Our fans were relentless in jeering John. They were pretty hard on Kenny when he played against us, but for John, the fans took booing to a new level.

Oklahoma State took a seven-point lead less than halfway into the first half. Our effort was relentless, and we kept Oklahoma State from running away from us. Terrance hit a late three, and when the buzzer sounded to end the first half, our fans were cheering like crazy. Trotting toward the locker room, I knew we had been playing well. I looked up at the scoreboard. We were tied 29–29.

Nucci gave us a brief lead starting the second half by turning a steal by Carl into a dunk. Oklahoma State immediately answered with a 14–2 burst and kept us at arm's length most of the rest of the way. But we had one last run in us.

A three by Terrance off a steal by Corey pulled us to within 67–65 with exactly a minute remaining. The Cowboys went up four with twenty-three seconds left. We scrambled to get off three three-point shots in the final six seconds, but we couldn't get one of them to fall. Oklahoma State's Tony Allen rebounded our last miss and heaved the ball the length of the court in relief. Somehow, the ball swished through the net for the final 72–65 score.

I approached John after the game. It was the final time we would see each other on the court. I didn't hug him, but I firmly shook his hand. I was so proud to be a Baylor Bear.

20

SAYING GOODBYE

Our last home game was against Kansas State. It was Senior Night, and the night I would break the Baylor career record for games played, with number 117, wearing my lucky 13.

I drove to the Ferrell Center earlier than usual and parked in the same spot I had for almost four years now. I sat in my car with mixed feelings as I stared at the gold-domed arena.

My vision for my Senior Night had been much different, and knowing we had reached our final two games brought so much finality. In my first three seasons, I did not know when or where our last game would take place. It could come in the first round of the Big 12 tournament, or the second or the third. We could earn a spot in the NCAA Tournament or NIT and finish our season in some arena or stadium around the country.

But this season had a definite endpoint. Since we were banned from the postseason, including the Big 12 tournament, I knew six months ago that my last home game would be Wednesday, March 3, against Kansas State and that the final game of my college career would be Saturday, March 6, at Oklahoma.

I made my routine visit to the training room for heat and electrical stimulation to loosen my neck and lower back. Then I took a seat in front of my locker. I had spent more than a thousand days in this locker room. I thought about some of the teammates who came and went. There had been thirty-four of them—more than most basketball programs because of the past year. I couldn't think of a better way to say goodbye to our fans than with a victory.

I was thankful to be sharing Senior Night with Terrance and R.T. If they hadn't stuck around, quitting would have been my best option.

In a pregame ceremony, the three of us were honored, along with our families. My parents were beside me as I received my framed jersey. Their sacrifices on my behalf started when I was in fourth grade. This was also my dad's 117th Baylor game.

Why not break the games-played record in style? The opening tip bounced free near the scorer's table. I took off after the ball, launched myself horizontally, flipped the ball back toward the court, and crashed over the table. The crowd stood and applauded as I trotted back around the table and onto the court. Though unscripted, that moment was how I would have liked the fans to remember me.

In our blowout loss in Stillwater, Oklahoma State had been the only team to exploit our zone defense with outside shooting. Kansas State joined OSU, shooting 66 percent from the field in taking a 39–22 halftime lead. I walked into the locker room angry. I couldn't accept going out by getting routed at home.

Coach Drew casually walked in.

"Pick your heads up," he said in a normal tone. I kept my head down—and, apparently, I wasn't the only one.

"Pick your heads up," he repeated.

Coach Drew was not a rah-rah guy. He didn't give *Hoosiers*-type speeches. He rarely needed to unload on us because effort wasn't our problem. Instead, he reminded us of team goals and the need to get back on track.

"All year long, you have kept fighting and not quit," he said. "You have gone through more than any team I know of. Don't stop now. Keep pushing. Let's get this closer, one possession at a time."

Ruining an opponent's Senior Night is satisfying, and Kansas State seemed intent on ruining ours. The Wildcats continued playing efficiently early in the second half. With 12:38 to play, we were down twenty-one, 53–32. Momentum is a crazy thing in sports, and especially in a fast-paced game like basketball. Once an opponent gains a little momentum, you have to stamp it out before it becomes unstoppable.

One step at a time. One possession at a time. Just chip away. That always was Coach's philosophy, and with each step, each possession, and each piece of K-State's lead we chipped away, momentum started snowballing.

Defensive stops led to easy buckets in transition. Off a steal, I split two defenders and—harkening back to my Pistol Pete videos days—dropped a no-look, behind-the-back pass to Corey for a layup that woke up the crowd.

Then I found Corey again for another basket.

Our defensive pressure intensified further. Inside the nine-minute mark, R.T. turned down a shot and swung the ball to me for a three-pointer. Coach Drew and our assistants pumped their fists and urged our crowd to make more noise. We were on our way to a 12–1 run that cut K-State's lead to single digits, 57–49, with under seven minutes to complete the comeback.

Our young players had come up big over and over again. On this night, at this point in the game, the seniors needed to step up. Coach Drew had placed so much trust in us, and we needed to show why he was correct to do so.

Our final push started at the 3:40 mark, from which we three seniors accounted for eleven of our final thirteen points. With us down seven, Terrance nailed a three-pointer that brought us within 61–57.

K-State tipped in a miss, and Tommy followed with a finish of his own to make the difference four points again. With fifty-nine seconds left, Coach called timeout and instructed us to pressure and go for the steal first, and then foul if we didn't get the ball. We fouled Cartier Martin. He made the first free throw and missed the second, leaving us still only two possessions behind. We were scripting a Hollywood movie in real-time. To be down by twenty-one, on our Senior Night, it felt only appropriate that we work our way back and win.

Terrance dribbled down the left side of the court. The 5,000 fans standing in the Ferrell Center sounded like 10,000. Terrance rhythm-dribbled several times, and when he had created enough separation from his defender, he released a shot from about five feet behind the left wing three-point arc. His shot looked bad, and I hustled to position myself for the coming rebound. But Terrance's shot found the perfect spot on the backboard and banked in. The crowd went insane as Coach Drew called another timeout. We rushed Terrance, who was looking up into the sky as though to say thanks for the help from the backboard— and perhaps from above.

With momentum and now luck on our side, this had to be our night for a storybook ending.

With thirty-nine seconds left, we trailed 64–62. We fouled on the inbounds pass and rebounded the missed free throw. The game was ours to tie or win.

I missed a difficult layup, forcing an off-balance shot off both feet while eluding two defenders. K-State rebounded the miss, and we fouled with fifteen seconds left. Once again, K-State missed the front end of a one-and-one. R.T. snagged the rebound, and I raced toward him to get the ball.

In a movie, the final fifteen seconds of a game like this one take about a minute to go by. That's only in the movies. These might have been the fastest fifteen seconds of my life.

I advanced the ball up the left side. A K-State defender tried to poke the ball away. Coach Drew could have called timeout, but he left it to us players to write the ending. I dribbled across half-court with eight seconds left. R.T. was standing at the right elbow. I attacked toward the middle of the paint, and R.T. moved out to the right wing. My defender cut me off, so I made a quick back exchange to get by him. Four seconds left.

R.T.'s defender sucker-helped on me just enough for me to kick the ball to R.T., our best three-point shooter. R.T. caught the pass as his defender quickly recovered. He faked a shot, dribbled once to his right, and let our last chance fly from the corner.

As bad as Terrance's earlier shot had looked, R.T.'s three-pointer looked equally good. From my angle, the ball was straight on line. I watched the ball bounce harmlessly off the rim.

I didn't move, standing there dumbfounded that R.T.'s shot hadn't gone in. A few of our guys fell to the floor in disbelief. I looked up into the crowd. Our fans were standing, applauding.

Senior Night always concluded with a postgame ceremony. As a player then and as a coach now, trust me when I say those ceremonies are tons more fun after a win.

Coach Drew addressed the crowd.

"First of all, to all of you who stayed and supported us all year long, we would like to clap for you."

"Tonight," he continued, "you saw the heart of the team and how we played all year long." The crowd interrupted with loud applause.

"The first half wasn't pretty by any means. But the second half, you saw a lot of heart and a lot of effort."

He paused as our fans applauded again.

"All this season, you have seen that these three seniors have laid the foundation for the future, and now all across the country, people know what Baylor basketball stands for."

Then it was time for the seniors to speak.

Terrance went first. I was standing to his right and saw his emotions on the verge of overtaking him.

"The situation last year got me so down on myself," he said. "I worked hard in the offseason to be a better player and a better person."

Someone in the crowd yelled, "You are!"

I was so glad I had witnessed Terrance's transformation from a self-centered whiner into an awesome teammate with contagious positivity. Terrance was directly responsible for helping me see any good in staying at Baylor. I hugged Terrance and thanked him for everything.

Coach Drew presented me with a basketball commemorating my career games played record. He handed me the microphone, and I struggled with how to describe my feelings. Part of me still wanted that ending with John, Lawrence, Kenny, and Patrick leading us into the Big 12 Tournament with me fulfilling the role for which I had prepared. I also wanted to give the crowd insight into how many unforgettable moments we had experienced this season, how miserable I had been, and the issues I still struggled with. How this team of leftovers had achieved more than I thought even the players would need time to realize. It wouldn't have been wise, though, to bare my soul in this setting. So, I thanked the fans for the four fantastic years they had given me as one of their Baylor Bears.

We were tired in the locker room following every game. This night, we felt the added emotional drain of our last home game plus a possible victory turned agonizing defeat. Most of us sat quietly at our lockers for a while. I got up to hug R.T., and then I made my way around the room, thanking my teammates individually.

Terrance and R.T. My fellow seniors. Man, we had walked through something together at a level very few people could experience.

Leaving the locker room was difficult. So many memories. I had shared this room with guys who were great teammates and some who weren't. We had lost more games than we won, but, no doubt, I had been a part of something much bigger than myself.

My reflection was halted by one of the great reasons for hope in athletics: the next game. Our season didn't have to end like this. We had one more opportunity. It wouldn't occur in the Ferrell Center, but we could still go out with a win.

Let's head to Norman, I thought, *and try to do what no one thinks we can do—one more time.*

PERFECT ENDING...FOR US

Truthfully, I was ready for the season to be over. The twenty-nine games over three and a half months had felt as long as my other three seasons combined. I was mentally and physically spent. My body occasionally balked at what I asked it to do. Averaging thirty-five minutes per game plus the stress in my life had taken its toll.

Thirteen months earlier, we had made this same four-hour bus trip to OU. If someone had told me that between that trip and this one, our team would be dismantled, our head coach disgraced, and all ours hope dashed, I would have replied, "Yeah, sure. Have another."

I replayed all the old events, starting with the police coming into our locker room looking for information about Patrick's whereabouts. Being questioned at the police station. Dottie's arrest. Patrick's body being found and his memorial service. The scandal around Coach Bliss. It was mindboggling to realize all that had happened in less than nine months.

My mind needed a break from the memories.

I looked out the window to the red dirt of Oklahoma. We had not beaten OU in my four years, and I couldn't recall a game when we gave them a scare. And no one was giving us any kind of a chance to win this game.

That's exactly how we liked it. What better sendoff than upsetting the Oklahoma Sooners on *their* Senior Night.

Our pregame rundown was much like the other twenty-eight games. Coach Drew was going over our team goals when he started getting a little more fired up than usual. We couldn't allow the Sooners to beat us on the boards, he told us. Then he raised his voice and yelled, "We will kick their ass on the boards tonight—and I will do pushups for that!"

He immediately dropped to the floor and knocked out ten explosive pushups for violating his no cursing rule. Every one of us players stood and cheered as he counted aloud each pushup.

Anyone walking past our locker room and hearing our shouting would have been baffled. What would an 8–20 team have to be so fired up about? The truth was, not much other than one more chance to compete. To look OU's starting five in the eye and say, "Let's go."

Before tipoff, our five starters huddled on the court, arms around each other's shoulders. I told them, "It's been an honor playing with you guys."

A small group of our fans had traveled to Norman, and we gave them plenty of plays to cheer in the first half. Harvey and I connected twice on long alley-oops. On both plays, I could sense the restlessness in the Sooners' crowd. Harvey and I laughed and slapped hands each time.

We kept the pace slow in the first half and excitedly sprinted toward our locker room for halftime down only two, 20–18.

We shocked the crowd even more by starting the second half with a 14–2 run. When our lead reached 32–22 at the 13:09 mark, OU coach Kelvin Sampson signaled a timeout. We believed we could win this game. We *deserved* to win.

But that's when the fatigue started setting in. We took poor shots. We gave up easy rebounds by not blocking out. We committed costly turnovers. In less than five minutes, the Sooners had erased their deficit, tying the score at 33, and their crowd was back in the game.

A timeout gave us a break to reset, and we retook the lead and held it for the next four minutes.

OU moved back in front, 40–39, with 2:49 left. We had learned in these situations to take on Coach Drew's demeanor. He was always positive and believing the impossible would happen, and that was our mindset on the court.

Two free throws gave the Sooners a three-point advantage, and then Terrance made a layup. I fouled to stop the clock at nineteen seconds, and OU made both free throws to go up three again. It was fitting to place the ball in Terrance's hands because he had been our most reliable scorer and a leader all season. He dribbled toward the right wing, and the ball ricocheted off his foot right and into an OU player's hands with eight seconds to go. Two more points for OU at the line, and the final buzzer sounded on our season. We lost 46–41.

That was it. My Baylor career was over. I accepted the idea that my basketball career was also over. I walked through the line shaking OU players' hands in almost a daze. Coach Sampson pulled me close to him. "If you want to get into coaching, let me know," he said. "I'll do anything I can to help."

I thanked him for the offer and made my last walk to our locker room.

Most of us sat at our lockers, heads down and elbows on our knees. I could hear a few sniffles. I was sad, angry, tired.

Coach Drew called for our attention. He thanked us for our never-ending effort and said we had instilled hope in the program.

Then Heath Nielsen spoke. As director of media relations, Heath was in our locker room after every game, waiting until the coaches finished talking and then taking a player or two to meet with the media. Heath was part of our family. But in all four of my seasons, he had never said a word during a postgame meeting.

On this night, he had something to say.

"You guys need to raise your heads," he said, "because you have nothing to be ashamed of. You made believers out of more people than you will ever know."

A long pause followed.

I don't think any of us understood the impact we had made on the Baylor community. I had often wondered if anyone cared that we continued to show up and play. Now, Heath was telling us that what we did mattered—and to many people.

I thought back to high school, when I'd had a total meltdown, crying and slamming lockers, after losing in the second round of the playoffs my senior year. *This* chapter-ending loss was much different. What a journey we had completed.

The coaches walked around the locker room, hugging their players. Coach Drew reminded each of us that we had established the foundation on which future teams could build. Baylor basketball had a bright future, he believed, because of us.

Outside the locker room, the waiting group of faithful family and friends greeted us. I held my mom and dad in long embraces. They had endured *everything* with me, each step of the way. All my pain and loss of hope, they had also felt. Whether we played at home or on the road, my dad had come to watch every single one of my 118 Baylor games. My family's support made it possible for me to finish what I had started four years earlier.

This team wasn't one to sit in silent reflection on the bus ride home. The time for ruminating was over! A walk-on had hidden a bottle of rum in his bag. When he broke out the bottle, we enjoyed each other's company, possibly for the last time. We celebrated all the way home, laughing and cutting up.

At one point, I told myself, "Only this group of leftovers could have handled this year the way we did."

We had earned this moment, and we had much to celebrate.

Together.

21

A STORY OF REDEMPTION

Our team wasn't completely shut out of the Big 12 tournament. I received an invitation to appear as a guest during the television halftime show of one of the games. So, a week later, I was inside the American Airlines Center again. But this time, I could only watch. At least I didn't have to pay for a ticket!

Part of me had wanted to decline, even though I was honored by the invitation. I was only one of the players who had played through the tragedy and scandal. All of us deserved to be at the tournament—in uniform, representing our school and playing. I decided to accept the interview to speak on my teammates' behalf. Plus, it would be my pleasure to tell the TV audience about my love for Baylor basketball and our school.

I loved being part of the tournament atmosphere. Oklahoma State was playing as I walked the length of the court, with John Lucas zipping around and wowing the crowd. Pat Knight grabbed my arm as I walked past. He was an assistant coach for his father at Texas Tech, and he made a few pleasant remarks about me and our team. I received numerous compliments about our team while at the tournament.

During the halftime show, the broadcasters' first questions were the ones I had answered what seemed like thousands of times throughout the season. I thanked Coach Drew and his assistants. I explained that he had brought us hope, and without the staff's great work, none of our accomplishments would have been possible. Their question that stung most was, "Do you look out and see the success that Lucas and Roberts are having and wonder, What if nothing had happened?" I had to hold back my distaste and give the answer I knew I should: I was proud of those guys and their success, and I wished them the best.

My retirement from basketball lasted two months. I was in the SLC one day and got roped into a pickup game. I quickly realized how much I missed playing. Through our marathon season, I had forgotten how much I loved basketball. The kid who spent thousands of hours practicing and dreaming was still alive inside me. My statistics were average, not great. I was a jack-of-all-trades and master of none, so I would be a hard sell to pro scouts. Coach Driscoll knew a scout in Iceland. He sent tape of me playing, and I received an offer to play on a team in the small town of Njardvik.

I had no idea they played basketball in Iceland, but I looked forward to a new start far away from the past. At the first practice, an Icelandic teammate asked where I played college ball. I told him I had graduated from Baylor. He looked perplexed, then asked in broken English, "Don't the basketball guys shoot guys there?" Even on that sparsely populated island nation in the North Atlantic, *it* followed me.

Our team won the Icelandic Championship that season, and at one point, I was rated the best point guard in the country. Unfortunately, drinking and partying were second nature in Iceland, and it was too easy for me to keep up my bad off-court habits. Basketball was not my highest priority, and my game suffered. As a result, that was my first and last professional season.

I returned from Iceland lost. I couldn't keep a job—I had nine over the span of three years.

Coach Thomas, my high school coach, helped me land work at a sports complex in the Dallas-Fort Worth area. My job included coaching a select team, and Coach T hoped coaching would reignite my passion for basketball. I was married, and when my wife became pregnant with our son Cade, I knew I needed to find a job with benefits. Coach T again tapped into his network for me, and in 2007, I took a full-time job as a reading teacher at Naaman Forest High School in Garland, where I could also serve as a volunteer assistant coach for head coach Jeff Clarkson. Cade made me a father while I was teaching and coaching there.

After one year at Naaman Forest, I accepted a job as an assistant coach for Wes Watson at McKinney High.

I was twenty-five, and Coach Watson spotted potential in me as a coach. He began grooming me to become a head coach, including turning over his team's offense to me. He also was a patient mentor for me on a personal level, which I sorely needed.

I could control a basketball offense, but I still couldn't control my life.

The damage was regrettable: a difficult divorce, a DWI, and too many broken relationships.

I had a hole in my life that I kept trying to fill with alcohol, women, working out, coaching, and anything else I thought might take my mind off my problems, even if only temporarily. My radio blared angry music to drown out my conscience. Anytime I allowed myself to think clearly, I experienced the same anxiety that caused me to dash out of that Fellowship of Christian Athletes meeting in a cold sweat years earlier.

I was still running in the wrong direction.

On any given night, with drink in hand, I would declare, "This is the last night! Tomorrow I start over!" Then after a few days of somewhat clean living, something triggered my anger and guilt, and I had to numb them.

Some nights I said, "If there is a God out there, please help me change!" But then I would choose to go right back to the same activities that were keeping me depressed. I rarely went to church, and when I did, my guilt prevented me from paying attention to the sermons.

Regret and shame accompanied me everywhere I went. I knew I was missing something, and I still chose the same solution—numb my pain. No matter what I tried, I could not find peace.

When people who knew me well started seeing through my cracks, I cut them out of my life. People like Steve Yoder, who had walked alongside me through seemingly everything. I could not call him because I didn't want him to know I was struggling.

I was living a lie.

One Sunday morning in November 2011, I decided to go to church. I liked the energy of the church's services and the pastor's messages when I did go, but I had no interest in connecting with any of the people. As usual, I took a seat in the back, hoping to sit unnoticed. The church had visitor's cards with spaces for a guest's name, contact information, and prayer requests or comments. I had not filled one out on any of my previous visits, but for some reason, I took a card.

In the space for comments, I wrote two things:

"I'm angry."

"I have questions."

I didn't expect a response. A few days later, I received an email from the church thanking me for filling out the card and offering an opportunity to meet with a pastor. By this point, I was open to anything that might help, but I believed the pastor was likely wasting his time.

After a few rounds of phone tag and because of my schedule as a basketball coach and the holidays, we set up a meeting in January.

On January 6, 2012—four days before my meeting with the pastor—I celebrated my thirtieth birthday alone with a six-pack in my apartment. I was miserable, asking myself, *Is this how my life is supposed to be? Is this all there is for me in life?*

When I walked into the church office, a woman greeted me and introduced herself as Jana. She had emailed me and helped to set up the appointment. I had pictured the email coming from the stereotypical image of an elderly church secretary. But Jana was a women's pastor at the church, about my age, and very attractive.

While we waited for the pastor, we sat and talked, and she asked me questions about my life. I was blown away by her kindness and her interest in hearing my story. She was much kinder to me than I was to myself back then.

I went into the meeting with the pastor with one goal in mind: I wanted to vent and explain why I was in the shape I was in. I poured out everything about Baylor, how I had faith growing up, and how I had been such a good kid. I told him I never imagined in high school that I could be sitting here as a thirty-year-old surrounded by hopelessness. The summer before my senior year at Baylor had put me on this roller-coaster ride, and I didn't know how to get off. I described how Pistol Pete, one of my heroes, had accepted Christ after injuries ended his NBA career and years of destructive behavior that followed. He was lying in bed when he heard a voice tell him that he was missing Jesus. Pistol Pete's life changed from that moment, and he lived the rest of his life doing amazing things for God.

I told the pastor, "I haven't heard anything."

"Don't be waiting for that," he told me. "It doesn't normally work that way."

My heart sank. I hadn't been able to straighten out on my own, and now I couldn't even hope for a Pistol Pete-like experience? Then where could I find the help I needed?

The pastor asked if I was saved, and I not so confidently answered that I had been saved since I was young.

His response froze me.

"Matt, you have to trust your salvation. Lean on Jesus to do the work in you. Stop those behaviors that are keeping you from reaching your potential."

I processed his statement in basketball terms: when I wanted to improve a part of my game, I had to spend time focusing on that area. *Could the same idea work for my relationship with God?*

The pastor explained that I could not earn my salvation; salvation was possible only through accepting Jesus as Lord and Savior. He also was direct in telling me that my life was out of control because of the decisions I had made at twenty-one. I had been avoiding accountability. *My decisions* caused my problems, not the circumstances at Baylor.

That one conversation changed my life.

The key word I took from our conversation was "surrender." I had been crying out for guidance without opening myself up to receive any. I had tried countless times to stop drinking, only to surround myself with alcohol. I demanded that God speak to me, but I was unwilling to read His Word or be in His house.

Finally, after nine years of chaos from living my way, I gave up.

I surrendered.

Immediately, peace overwhelmed me. Paul describes it as a peace that *"transcends all understanding"* (Philippians 4:7).

Before my senior year at Baylor, I believed faith was the foundation of my life. I had grown up in church and could probably score well on a Bible test. I was vocal about my faith; I was living and acting as a

Christian should. I was known as a basketball player *and* a Christian. But I didn't realize that the essence of Christianity is not calling yourself a Christian and trying to be good. It's a relationship with Jesus Christ and making Him Lord of your life. The tragedy and the scandal at Baylor revealed I had built my life around basketball. *That* was my idol. And when the source of my identity got ripped away, I had nothing.

From the day I met with the pastor, I never had the desire to party or drink alcohol again. With God's help, my last drink occurred on my thirtieth birthday. I started attending church regularly and serving as a volunteer. I studied the Bible, which drew me closer to God. I changed the types of TV shows I watched and the music I listened to. I was amazed at how listening to worship music in the morning affected the rest of my day.

Before my senior year, I had behaved how I knew I should and said the things I knew I needed to say. I was trying to live a Christian life out of my knowledge. But now, I lived out of an authentic love for God and appreciation for His faithfulness to me. I was living from the outflow of a changed heart.

Looking back, I can see God's plan bringing me to a place where I would meet someone who would change the trajectory of my life. But that person wasn't the pastor!

Before I left the church that day, Jana gave me her phone number and offered the church's help with any of my needs or questions. Her offer wasn't a hey-I'm-interested-in-you type of offer. And I was trying to find myself, not a wife. But Jana genuinely cared for me and wanted to make sure I understood the church's desire to help me spiritually.

I texted her later that day to thank her for helping to arrange my meeting with the pastor.

Jana and I began to exchange texts, and then we started calling each other. Over a three-day period, we spent thirteen hours on the phone! She listened to my story, and I listened to hers. She also was divorced

and had a son, Landon. A few weeks later, we met up for a friend date...
and the rest of that story is easy to figure out.

We married that December.

Before meeting Jana, I had convinced myself that because of my
past, I could never find a godly woman who would want to love me. I
believed my sins were worse than others' because I had grown up in
church and knew all along I was living the wrong way. I knew the truth,
and I had chosen to reject God.

I could not have been more wrong.

FINDING MY CALLING

My coaching style changed when my lifestyle changed.

When I was frustrated and upset about my life, I brought my personal issues into how I coached. I had failed to recognize the ways in
which I was more Bliss than Drew as a coach. I got upset with our players too easily. I maintained a transactional approach toward them.

My mindset toward my players was, *What can you do for me?*
Nothing? Then get out of the way. Next guy up!

I became a coach because I had played basketball since I was nine
and loved the game. After recommitting my life to Christ, my coaching
became about relationships.

I started a morning Bible study for any player who wanted to attend.
We read through Tony Dungy's book, *Uncommon*. For the first time in
my life, faith and basketball were connected.

In the spring of 2013, after five years as an assistant coach, I was
ready to become a head coach. The McKinney school district had three
high schools, and Boyd—the district's newest and largest school—
needed a head coach. I was told the job was mine if I wanted it.

Jana and I prayed, and we decided not to pursue the opening.

Coach Thomas called and told me I was making a mistake. I had no head coaching experience, he reminded me, and had turned down the head job at a high school in Texas's largest classification. Such an opportunity might never again come my way. After talking with my trusted mentor, I wondered if I had made the wrong decision.

But after Jana and I prayed some more, we felt reassured about our decision.

Two weeks later, Randy Feemster, a friend who coached at a large private school, called and told me about a Christian school in Dallas-Fort Worth that needed a head coach. I had not been interested in coaching at a private school because at McKinney, we had a bad experience with a private school attempting to recruit our players away from us.

"Take a look and let me know what you think," Coach Feemster told me.

The school was Grapevine Faith Christian School. I checked out the school's website and loved what I read about the school's mission to educate kids through a biblical worldview. I called Coach Feemster and told him I was interested, and he said he would put in a recommendation for me.

I was invited to an interview with four of the school's top administrators. Although I had never interviewed for a head coach's position, I felt confident about the basketball part. At McKinney, we ran a fast-paced, running-and-gunning, three-point-shooting offense paired with a high-pressure defense. We had an attractive style of basketball to play and to watch. I put together a binder filled with information about how I would transform Faith's boys' basketball program into that style.

But I was terrified about the non-basketball part of the interview. I could not figure out how to reveal my past. Some old thoughts came back, and I determined all I needed to do was put on a good show for the administrators, telling them exactly what they wanted to hear.

The drive to Grapevine was thirty-five minutes or so—about long enough to listen to a sermon podcast. Jana and I were attending a different church than where we met, and I picked out a recent sermon by a guest speaker there.

I arrived at the school a little early, and the sermon wasn't quite over, so I stayed in my car to listen to more of it. The speaker told the congregation, "You have to stop giving edited testimonies because they do nothing for no one."

Wow!

I could not have heard that message at a better time. In the parking lot, I changed my plan and decided to tell the administrators who I was, the mistakes I had made, and—most importantly—what God had done in my life.

During the interview, I told the administrators, "I don't know exactly what I am supposed to tell you." Then I recounted the line from the sermon I had just heard and told my story from Baylor up to the present.

I got the job.

Nine years later, as I write this book, I am still head coach of the Grapevine Faith Lions. I also teach physical education.

Coaching used to be transactional for me. Now, it's transformational.

I am not coaching just to help my players become better at scoring. If they already have a relationship with Christ, my job is to help them develop a stronger one. If they don't, I plant seeds that I pray will grow and, one day, those players will accept Christ. And that has happened.

My focus is not on developing complete players but complete young men.

I am demanding but not demeaning, and I am still as competitive as ever. It's okay for Christians to compete hard. I believe we have the best reason to be competitive!

I coach my players to play hard and bring their best to every practice and game. I'm no different than any coach in that regard. But I have noticed that we coaches tend not to tell why we push our players to be their best. As a Christian, the *why* goes back to the cross. Christ gave His life for us on the cross, and our teams strive to represent Him in everything we do.

During my senior year at Baylor, I failed to be a light. One of our program goals at Grapevine Faith is to be a light in the basketball community. When people watch our team—regardless of whether we win or lose—I hope they see how hard we play, how we interact with one another, how coachable our players are, and the joy in our players and coaches. We want them to notice something different about Faith basketball.

JAMODI is a significant part of our program, but it's a different concept than the one that pushed me through my high school and college playing days. I came to see some flaws in the concept of "Just A Matter Of Doing It." Real life was not a matter of just doing it. Otherwise, everyone could work hard and get precisely what they wanted from life.

So, at Faith, I created a new-and-improved JAMODI: Joy, Attitude, Motivation, Opportunity, Determination, and Impact.

Through JAMODI, joy is bringing energy and spirit. Coach Drew told us that "JOY" stood for "Jesus, Others, and then You." When we think first thing in the morning about Christ dying for us on the cross so His blood would redeem us, how can we not have joy that day? We start the day with joy, and that changes our attitude for the rest of the day. When our attitude is correct, we choose to be motivated. Many players do not want to be motivated because that requires being challenged and facing obstacles to overcome. Too many people wake up in the morning wanting no challenges to come their way that day. We embrace challenges because they help us grow. When we are motivated, our eyes are open to opportunities all around us that might otherwise go unseen.

I wrote this book during our second season of dealing with COVID-19. As horrible as the pandemic has been, it still has presented opportunities. For high school players who rely on coaches to tell them what to do, it had been easy to stay on the couch. But our players have goals and strong work ethics; they have improved their skills themselves through their driveway and backyard baskets. Next, when we see opportunities, we determine to accomplish them. Obstacles allow us to see how much we want to achieve our goal. Then when we follow through, we are able to impact others—and that is the reason we are here.

JAMODI also applies to me as a coach.

I need to bring joy to my team every day, and my joy comes from remembering the cross. I also want my players to see that I am excited to coach them. Players follow my attitude, and my attitude after a loss is, "Next!" Next practice, next game—let's learn and get better. I will not dwell on the past. I am motivated every day to be the very best for myself and also as a competitor. As a coach, we face all kinds of problems with our players, such as illnesses, bad grades, injuries, and difficult losses. These problems are opportunities. The school gym is unavailable today? Fine, that gives us an opportunity to improve by watching game film or talking about our faith as a group. I used to get frustrated when *my* plans didn't go the way *I* wanted. Now, I recognize that God is in control of everything, so it's useless to get bent out of shape when I do not get what I want. I am determined to teach through whatever comes our way because almost every moment in sports can lead to teaching that helps my players in their lives. Practically, that means focusing on relationships so I know what my players are feeling and going through. I can't allow myself to look at them as pieces on a chessboard. I want to impact the relationships God has entrusted me with through basketball. Billy Graham said, "A coach will impact more people in one year than the average person will in an entire lifetime." Coaching is a unique calling, and I need to make sure I go into every day asking, "How can I impact my players?"

I see my players in their rawest forms at times, and I want them to know I value them as people too. I tried playing basketball while always striving to please my coaches. I also tried living performance-based spirituality.

Other people do not determine your value. God does. Today's youth desperately need to hear this message from us and see it demonstrated through us.

And they need to know that God's love is unconditional.

22

THE FOUNDATION

I was unsure how to respond when asked if I would like to see Coach Bliss.

I was an assistant at McKinney High, and our head coach received an invitation to hear Bliss teach at a coaches' clinic in north Dallas. I'd had no contact with Coach Bliss since the day he announced his resignation to the team.

"Sure, why not?" I answered.

I didn't know what to expect when I saw Coach, and I was a little guarded going into the meeting room. When Coach and I made eye contact, he looked happy to see me and embraced me.

The moment Coach started talking basketball, I fell right back into that love of hearing him teach the sport. He was a brilliant basketball mind, and he still had his "A" game as a speaker. But I also was sad because fewer than ten coaches had come to hear him.

Coach transitioned into his personal story. He admitted making mistakes, owning not only what he had done wrong the summer before my senior year but also in the years before as a coach. When he said he had allowed the pressures of his job to get to him, he didn't seem to be offering an excuse. He genuinely sounded like a man telling his story as an example to help prevent other coaches from repeating his mistakes.

After that day, Coach and I communicated with each other now and then to keep in touch. The NCAA had imposed a ten-year "show-cause penalty" on Coach, which would attach penalties against him to any NCAA program that hired him. He was practically untouchable to NCAA schools. He had returned to coaching at a college preparatory school in Texas.

During the fall semester of 2013, a week before the start of practices for my first season at Grapevine Faith, Coach emailed to say he was coming to my area and would like to talk with me.

"Sure, Coach," I responded. "Whenever you want."

He suggested a week from that day. I told him that would be the first day of practice with my new team, but I could meet with him. Coach said he also would like to observe our practice.

Not only would Coach and I have our first real conversation since Baylor, but one of the top basketball minds in the country also would be at my very first practice as a head coach!

We met in my office, and Coach said he wanted to apologize for "everything I put you through at Baylor." I saw tears in his eyes as he said he felt horrible about his mistakes. He admitted that he was supposed to lead us and he had failed to do so. His remorse was real.

I told him I forgave him.

Coach watched our practice and, afterward, he went over a few helpful notes he had written out for me.

"I am so proud of you," he told me. "You're going to be a great coach."

The following year, he came to see me at my school again for a short visit. I asked him to talk to my team before practice, and he was as impactful as back in the days of those FCA meetings we spoke at together.

I was thrilled to see Coach using his story for good.

In late 2016, I was contacted by a group filming a documentary about the Baylor scandal entitled *Disgraced*. They asked if they could interview me, and I said sure.

The interview lasted two and a half hours, and near the end, I had noticed their focus was on the summer's events. I asked if we could talk about the leftovers and my senior year; to me, that was the real story. They obliged, although none of that portion of the interview made it into the documentary.

Disgraced aired on Showtime in March 2017, almost fourteen years since the longest summer, and Jana watched it with me. I had felt stupid and naïve back then after learning that drug use and cheating were going on around me without my knowledge. I learned even more watching the documentary.

The crucial part of the documentary for me—as I'm sure it was for most viewers—came during part of the interview with Coach Bliss. He was coaching at a small Christian university in Oklahoma at the time, and I thought he had handled the interviewer's questions pretty well. I was sensing the same remorse that I had felt from him when we visited in my office. Then at one point, Coach must have assumed the camera was off or that he was speaking off the record.

For some reason, he started making absurd comments about Patrick Dennehy.

Coach said Patrick sold drugs to "all the white guys on campus." He called Patrick "a druggie" and said, "He was the worst." Coach portrayed himself as a victim, concluding that portion of the interview with, "I got in the mud with the pigs, and I paid a price. And the pigs liked it."

I couldn't understand why Coach would dig up old claims when investigations by Waco police, the university, and the NCAA had never found one piece of evidence that Patrick was a drug dealer. As Coach talked about Patrick, he came across as someone who had told himself a lie so many times that he had come to believe it to be true.

Three weeks after the documentary aired, Coach resigned from the university where he was coaching.

He and I haven't talked or exchanged an email or text since the day he spoke to my players.

In the three years I played for Coach Bliss, I desperately wanted to get close to him, to get to know him better. I couldn't figure him out. I still can't.

COMPLETING THE TURNAROUND

After I drank away my professional career, I didn't attempt to reconnect with Coach Drew or the Baylor basketball program.

My exit from basketball in Iceland was disgraceful, and I was also part of a dark chapter in Baylor's history. I remembered how I felt my senior season attempting to move forward while people kept dredging up the past. I figured I represented an era at Baylor that everyone wanted to distance themselves from.

I didn't know if the season with the leftovers mattered.

Three years after leaving Baylor, I returned to the Ferrell Center to watch a game. I feared what I might hear or see if someone recognized me. Thankfully, I made it through the game without being noticed.

Afterward, I walked down to the floor to relive some of the good memories, to see how it felt to have the court beneath my feet once more. Coach Drew was at the far end of the court; I had no plans to approach him or try to attract his attention. Yet I looked up to see him almost sprinting across the floor toward me with a broad smile and his arms wide open. I still get teary when I recall the sight of him approaching me.

When he got to me, he pulled me into a firm embrace.

"I am so happy to see you," he told me.

He made me feel like I had played for him for four years.

We chatted a little bit, and at the end of our conversation, even though we said goodbye, I had the feeling I would hear from him again.

My return to the Ferrell Center came during the season in which Baylor's program appeared to have fully recovered from the sanctions. Based on the NCAA's favorable response to Baylor's self-imposed sanctions, the university's swift and decisive action might have saved our program from the death penalty.

The NCAA extended the probation period until 2010, banned the team from playing nonconference games during the 2005–06 season, and reduced paid recruiting visits for 2006–07, plus a few more minor penalties. In announcing the sanctions, the NCAA said, "The coaches' disregard for NCAA rules has tarnished them, the university, and intercollegiate athletics as a whole."

The NCAA didn't kill the program, but it severely crippled Baylor basketball. Somehow, Coach Drew and his staff already had our program ready to take off.

The following year—the 2007–08 season—Baylor won twenty-one games and made the school's long-awaited return to the NCAA Tournament. Each time Baylor achieved a milestone victory, Coach texted a group of us former players to let us know about the win and the role we played in rebuilding the program.

In December 2010, Baylor played Gonzaga at American Airlines Center in Dallas. We had won twenty-eight games the season before and advanced to the Elite Eight. I attended the game with no concern about being recognized or connected to a time best forgotten. I still didn't know, though, if fans cared about the team from my senior season.

I walked down the steps of the arena wearing a Baylor basketball T-shirt. To my surprise, not only did fans recognize me, but a few stood to shake my hand and thank me for my years at Baylor.

About ten rows from the floor, I stopped and looked at the Baylor team below me. The players were huge! (Two, Perry Jones and Quincy Acy, went on to play in the NBA.) The team my senior year had average-looking guys at best. I couldn't believe the difference.

Mark Wible, the team chaplain, spotted me and waved for me to join him. Pastor Wible was a six-foot-eight bear of a guy, and when he hugged me, he *really* hugged me.

"Look out at the floor," he told me, pointing to our players. "We would not be here if not for what you guys did Coach Drew's first year."

I felt my lip quivering and blood rushing to my face.

At dinner after the game, a man approached me.

"Are you Matt Sayman?" he asked.

"I am," I said.

He reached out to shake my hand.

"I appreciate you sticking around back then."

Coach Drew had infused Baylor basketball with hope. And the leftovers had not been forgotten.

Jana, Cade, Landon, and I had started driving down to Waco to attend more games. Each time, soaking in the Ferrell Center atmosphere and being around the program again, felt right.

Coach Drew invited me to talk with his team about my senior year during the 2018–19 season. Baylor had made seven NCAA Tournament appearances under him by that time and had been ranked number one in the nation for the first time in program history.

The locker room had received an upgrade. The gear set out for the players blew my mind. During my time, we received one T-shirt, one set of gear for practice, and one pair of shoes for the season. I estimated eight or nine pairs of shoes in lockers, not to mention what looked like full wardrobes. I thought I had entered the big time when I played college basketball, but *this* was big time.

I could tell the players had familiarity with the program's history, and they appreciated me being there to meet with them.

That team won twenty games and lost in the second round of the NCAA Tournament. I believed the next season's team was the best Baylor had put together and had the potential to make it to the Final Four, if not win the championship. They had a 26–4 record and had been ranked in the nation's top five all season when COVID-19 cut the season short before the start of the Big 12 tournament.

But nothing—not a pandemic, not undefeated Gonzaga—could stop us from winning the 2020–21 national championship.

Coach Drew made sure former players were invited to the championship celebration in Waco, and he didn't limit the invites to players who had played for him. I met players from the 1970s, '80s, and '90s. When I played, I knew nothing about the players from previous decades. We were never given a reason to feel connected to them. Now, Coach Drew was including at least fifty years' worth of former players in the celebration. Our program had been fractured for decades, and he had turned Baylor basketball into a family.

I was part of a dinner at Buzzy Billy's, where we ate our team meals before home games under Coach Bliss. We had dreamed back then of being the team to make Baylor history, and on this night, I was able to hold the program's first national championship trophy. Landon posed for photos with Coach Drew and Jared Butler, the Most Outstanding Player of the Final Four.

The highlight of the celebration was a parade in downtown Waco.

Former players participated in the parade, walking ahead of the vehicles carrying the current players. From the team of leftovers, Terrance, Tommy, Robbie, and Turner were on hand. R.T. couldn't make it because he was overseas. Fans lining the streets of the parade route knew who we were and expressed their appreciation. Just like me, the other leftovers had come to understand that they were part of the foundation. It would not be an exaggeration to say that through the years, the number of fans who have thanked me for staying at Baylor numbers in the hundreds.

Being a leftover wasn't easy. When people learn I played college basketball, they ask where and when. Then their eyes show their minds connecting the dots—and the same batch of questions typically ensues. Was that when that player got murdered? Were you on *that* team? Did you know what was going on?

I try to shift the conversations to basketball and the team during my senior year. At some point, they ask about our record.

"We were 8–21," I say.

At that point, I usually hear some version of, "I'm sorry."

"It was not a failure of a season," I tell them. "It was the most success I'd ever had."

That response always puzzles them. Who could understand unless they were one of the leftovers? And as my teammates and I walked toward the end of the parade route, where the largest group of fans was awaiting the big championship ceremony, I was surrounded by four guys who understood.

I had to work to fight back the tears.

We were an outmanned group of leftovers who took the court each game just trying to be competitive. It was hard. I wanted to quit. I lost control of my life.

But now, alongside Terrance, Tommy, Robbie, and Turner, we weren't only celebrating a national championship team—we were *part* of the national championship team. We were the foundation.

And, finally, more than seventeen years after the season I never wanted, I could answer the question that had shadowed me since.

Yes, it was worth it.

ABOUT THE AUTHORS

Matt Sayman received a full athletic scholarship to play basketball at Baylor University from 2000–2004. After remaining with the program following a shocking scandal in the off-season before his senior year, Matt broke the Baylor career record for games played (118). He then played professional basketball in Iceland, winning the Icelandic championship for Njardvik in 2005.

Matt is currently the varsity basketball coach at Grapevine Faith Christian School in Texas, where he has led his team to the state semi-finals the past two seasons. He enjoys inspiring young athletes with a message of "no magic"—just hard work, dedication, and a determination to work harder than the next guy.

Matt also serves as director of events for MGBasketball camps, where he is known for his ability to connect and inspire young athletes to give their best and improve each day.

He hosts JAMODI (Just A Matter Of Doing It) podcast, in which he interviews coaches and leaders to explore the reasons behind their successes.

Matt and his wife Jana live near Fort Worth, Texas, with their two sons.

David L. Thomas is the author or co-writer of more than a dozen books. He collaborated on two *New York Times* bestsellers: *Foxcatcher* with Mark Schultz and *Wrestling for My Life* with Shawn Michaels. In addition, *All In* with Gene Chizik was a *Wall Street Journal* national bestseller, and *SEAL of God* with Chad Williams surpassed 100,000 copies in print. Four of David's books have been or are in the process of being made into feature-length films.

David spent almost three decades in sports journalism, most recently as a senior writer and sports humor columnist for the *Fort Worth Star-Telegram*. There, his work was honored nationally by the Associated Press Sports Editors, and he received the McClatchy Company President's Award for excellence in journalism. David also worked for *The Dallas Morning News*. A lifelong Texan and graduate of the University of Texas at Arlington, he lives near Fort Worth, Texas, and may be reached at davidthomasauthor.com.